W0037977

PROUD PROPERTY OF

Quarto.com

© 2025 Quarto Publishing Group USA Inc.
Text © 2025 Nicole Coenen

First Published in 2025 by Cool Springs Press, an imprint of The Quarto Group,
100 Cummings Center, Suite 265-D, Beverly, MA 01915, USA.
T (978) 282-9590 F (978) 283-2742

All rights reserved. No part of this book may be reproduced in any form without written permission of the copyright owners. All images in this book have been reproduced with the knowledge and prior consent of the artists concerned, and no responsibility is accepted by producer, publisher, or printer for any infringement of copyright or otherwise, arising from the contents of this publication. Every effort has been made to ensure that credits accurately comply with the information supplied. We apologize for any inaccuracies that may have occurred and will resolve inaccurate or missing information in a subsequent reprinting of the book.

Cool Springs Press titles are also available at discount for retail, wholesale, promotional, and bulk purchase. For details, contact the Special Sales Manager by email at specialsales@quarto.com or by mail at The Quarto Group, Attn: Special Sales Manager, 100 Cummings Center, Suite 265-D, Beverly, MA 01915, USA.

29 28 27 26 25   1 2 3 4 5

ISBN: 978-0-7603-9267-6

Digital edition published in 2025
eISBN: 978-0-7603-9268-3

Library of Congress Cataloging-in-Publication Data available.

Design: Landers Miller Design
Page Layout: Landers Miller Design
Photography: Melanie Orr Photography, Nicole Coenen, and Shutterstock (See page 194 for more details.)

Printed in China

The information in this book is for educational purposes only. Proper safety gear should always be worn and proper precautions should always be taken when working with wood or with an axe. The author and publisher disclaim any liability from the reader's failure to follow proper safety precautions.

AXE
IN
HAND

A WOODCHOPPER'S GUIDE
TO BLADES, WOOD,
AND FIRE

Nicole Coenen

COOL
SPRINGS
PRESS

CONTENTS

INTRODUCTION

WELCOME TO THE WOODCHOPPER'S GUIDE TO AXES, BLADES, AND FIREWOOD!

I'm thrilled to take you on this journey that stretches back millions of years to the origin of the axe and its deep-rooted place in human history. Together, we'll learn about how the axe evolved in our hands, remaining an essential tool in our daily lives. This book will also take us into the heart of the forest where we'll get more acquainted with our local ecosystems and how we can work in partnership with them to create a more self-sufficient lifestyle. Together, we will explore various firewood tasks and activities, from the methodical art of woodchopping, to effectively storing wood for optimal burning. We'll also dive into methods for building a reliable fire in order to best enjoy the simple pleasure of roasting marshmallows with friends.

When you get lost in something bigger than yourself, you can discover so much more about who you can be.

I spent most of my younger years growing up in the suburbs outside a metropolitan area, yet had a constant draw to the forest. The forest became a place to explore my natural curiosities and expand the realm of discovery. My childhood house was down the road from a small, forested wetland area. I have some early memories of walking down to that forest on my own and venturing into the woods with no plan or end destination, just being led by the pull of the wild —even if it was a very tame and curated "wild." As I stepped onto the wooded trail, sheltered by the canopy of trees, with songs of the birds filling the air, breathing in the scent of the marsh and the soft, raw earth beneath my feet, I always found a deep sense of peace. It felt like I was exactly where I needed to be. I still get that feeling whenever I am immersed in a natural space. It's as if the rest of the world turns off and all expectations, judgments, and worries are silenced. Although the forest is always evolving, it still feels like returning home to a familiar place. And even if it's not the same forest you often visit, once you've connected with one, you feel connected to them all.

Throughout every stage of my life, in every challenge or celebration, the forest has always been a place for comfort, clarity, and adventure. Maybe you also have some memories of heading to the woods to build stick forts with friends. Or maybe you found yourself wandering off a trail to do some solo wildlife observations, or perhaps you feel drawn to the ambience of a forest as a place for-rest. There is so much you can awaken in yourself and the world around you when you follow that draw to nature. I bet you'll be surprised by all it has to show you. When we work with nature to aid us in our own survival, such as in the ways of harvesting trees for firewood, we are invited to learn more about these natural resources and how we can be better stewards of them. Through deeper learning and connecting, we can be a part of helping to strengthen and protect nature. For our local communities, the planet, and future generations.

If you've picked up this book, maybe you already have a connection with the trees in your region or maybe you're curious about getting into your woods. Whatever brought you here, we are going to celebrate the timeless draw humans have to get back to nature and deepen our appreciation for all the things the natural world provides. Whether you're a seasoned woodchopper or a curious beginner, you'll find stories, tips, and knowledge contained within these pages. Maybe even a few laughs along the way.

"AXE-PERT"

You might be wondering: "Why is she writing a book about axes and fire-wood?" To be honest, I didn't grow up chopping firewood and my family of six wasn't really a camping kind of family. I only remember holding an axe once in my childhood and I don't even think I was allowed to try swinging it. I was always drawn to nature, but my relation-ship with the forest felt very passive and separated from the rest of my life. When I was living in a city, I would often go to the forest with my dog on long walks; it became the highlight of our day. I would feel very connected while I was there, noticing the seasonal changes of the leaves, the different smells that would amplify after a rainstorm and how my body would breathe deeper while I was there. But once I got back to my noisy city apartment, the forest felt like a distant world. I also realized I was very limited in my knowledge of how to connect my lifestyle to the forest and how to create an active partnership with it. Finally, when I was in my late twenties, I had enough of city life and made the move to a small mountain town in the interior of British Columbia. I went from working at a remote desk job to waking up at 4:30 a.m. to go milk goats and get my hands dirty on a small family-run farm. It was a big learning curve, but I loved every minute of it. Working with the land to grow food and raise animals fosters a desire to deepen one's understanding of the land's needs. When you're trying to learn about a subject that's as expansive and broad as sustainable farming, it can be overwhelming when trying to figure out where to start. But there's a guide you already have right in front of you: the land itself. Through attentiveness, you can notice the behaviors of the plants, the influence of the weather, and the changes in the soil. The land is constantly telling us what it needs; we just need to learn to listen.

One of the tasks on the farm was chopping firewood. If you'd seen the way I swung that axe back then, you'd probably discourage me from ever pick-ing up an axe again. However, I was determined to prove I could do these

kinds of labor-based tasks. So, I kept swinging and eventually the swings became chops.

After a few years of living in small mountain towns in the interior, I moved to a small island in the Pacific Northwest. The cabin I moved into, which was owned by friends of mine, had a little woodstove, and we shared firewood piles to heat our homes. My friends suggested I join the Green Angel Woodchoppers, a local woodchopping group, to get involved in the community and do some physical activity. At the time I connected with them, the group was mainly composed of older men who had been chopping wood for half my lifetime. The Green Angels source local trees that have been downed by a storm or felled on private properties and the owners want the wood removed. We then go to buck and chop the trees into firewood. The firewood is then sold and the revenue from the wood is donated to various community initiatives. Sometimes, the wood is donated directly to people who need it for winter heating. I learned so much from that group. When I first joined, my axe swings were so clumsy and aimless. The more experienced choppers would give me tips and tricks and, eventually, I was able to power up my swing and build my accuracy.

Eventually, I learned about the internet's fascination for woodchopping and that has taken my life in a wild direction. It all started one day when I was doom scrolling through TikTok. I came across a video of a guy named Thoren Bradley chopping a big round of wood. It was impressive and people in the comments seemed to love it. For some reason, I thought it would be funny to do a spoof of this guy. I've always liked making videos as a creative outlet, so I went out to the chopping block in the yard to film my Thoren Bradley spoof. I posted that video to my TikTok, which had less than 1,500 followers at the time. After posting the video, I didn't really think much of it. To my surprise, that video started to gain traction and got a pretty good response. So, I did another "dramatic" woodchopping video, then another. Eventually, I stopped spoofing Thoren Bradley (who is an incredible chopper and human, shout-out to Thoren!) and I did my own spin on things.

Things kept growing from there. Within eight months, I became a full-time content creator. I had never set out to do this for a living, but I kept having fun with it and loved the opportunities this niche started to expand into. After holding many axes in my hands and breaking more than a few handles through the years, I began to experiment with different renovation techniques, which led me to explore more about how axes are made. I've been lucky enough to work with master blacksmiths who have guided me through the process of taking a chunk of metal and crafting it into a razor-sharp axe. The more you work with an old tool, the more its historic and cultural significance begins to reveal itself. I'm still discovering more every day and am constantly surprised about how this seemingly simple tool has such a profound legacy that continues to unfold into this modern era.

So, if you're ready to sharpen up your axe and head into the woods, then let's "em-bark" on this adventure together.

WOOD
AS HEAT

* * *

Firewood still remains a significant heat source for millions of households, whether as a primary or supplementary source. Especially in rural areas where access to other energy sources may be unreliable or more expensive, having a large stack of firewood will bring a lot of reassurance for those colder months. Wood burning can also be a preference for some people who want to utilize their self-sufficiency skills and strengthen their tie to nature. Whatever path led you to the wood stack, you'll realize it's a labor of love that will transfer to a warm and cozy home.

CHAPTER 1

THE AXE: CARVING A PLACE IN HISTORY

How powerful do you feel when you pick up an axe? Answers may vary. Some people pick up an axe and immediately feel super confident, comfortable, and ready to don some flannel and head to the forest. Others pick one up and it feels awkward in their hands; they don't know what to do with it, how to properly hold it, or its range of uses. There's no one-size-fits-all formula for becoming confident with an axe, but I can say there are two things that make all the difference: hands-on practice (a.k.a. actually using an axe) and solid, good old-fashioned knowledge. While this chapter won't get you swinging just yet (that's what chapter 2 is for), by the end, you'll know your axe's butt from its knob and have a deeper appreciation for how this chunk of metal and wood became the powerful tool it is today.

IN THIS CHAPTER

The axe is a pretty impressive tool, backed by thousands of years of history. In fact, the first stone axe was discovered to be used more than 1 million years ago by our *Homo erectus* ancestors. That means it's one of the oldest tools still used by modern humans.

To me, what's just as impressive is that as you look over the history of the axe, you also see so many uses: wood-splitting, hunting, wood carving, trading, fighting, sporting activities, religious ceremonies . . . yes, the axe has truly carved a place for itself in our history books. Even the axe we know today, the metal blade attached to a wooden—most likely hickory or ash—handle, has gone through many different forms and functions during its evolution to better suit its purposes. Based on which materials were available for its makers and what people were trying to use it for, there are a surprising number of styles, patterns, and builds.

In this chapter, I cover both the common and the uncommon forms of the axe, focusing on models still available to buy new or used today. We'll also take a look at some key axe history, axe anatomy, and more. By the end, you should be better able to find the axe that's the perfect fit for you and answer a bunch of axe-related questions at your next trivia night.

AXES THROUGH TIME

First, let's dive into some history. Why might you want to know the history of this seemingly simple inanimate object? You might have general curiosity or you might be fascinated to find that these tools are intrinsic when it comes to the evolution of humanity. In fact, when

A symbol of strength and balance: The labrys, an ancient double-headed axe, carries the weight of history and empowerment.

you look at the milestones of early tool development and human brain growth, it's a feedback loop.

When we first started building tools, we used the resources around us to help with our daily tasks, such as harvesting food and building shelter. When we had more food, our brains could grow faster and stronger. With better brain capacity, we could come up with new ways to create even better tools. When we had better tools, we could harvest more food, and the cycle continued.

According to the Smithsonian Institution, the earliest stone tools date back to 2.6 million years ago, when early humans began using stones for tasks such as butchering, digging, and cutting. These early stone tools then began to advance in their design. The first stone handaxe was found in Kenya and dates back to 1.76 million years ago.

The more we developed these tools, the more we developed our brain. We built these tools and these tools also helped build us. Let's explore a few of these early axes.

Handaxe

Some early handaxes, such as the Acheulean handaxes, were carved from silica-rich stone, including flint, chert, and rhyolite. They took on a teardrop shape with a pointed edge. Later these handaxes were made from antlers and bones. Early humans would shape these handaxes by knapping (striking the edge of the stone to remove flakes) using a "hammerstone" (a tougher stone) until the carved stone reached its desired shape with a sharper edge on one end. The process of knapping is similar to breaking glass, which as you can imagine can be like trying to control chaos.

While Acheulean handaxes are associated with our *Homo erectus* ancestors, Neanderthals had their own build of handaxes known as the Mousterian. The Mousterian is very similar to the Acheulean handaxe in look and usage but its manufacturing is a bit more complex. The Neanderthal had a similar process of selecting a stone and chipping or "knapping" flakes off the stone with a hammerstone, which was a stronger, more durable stone. Experts say that the Neanderthal seemed to have a bit more intention in their silica-rich stone selection and would sometimes make multiple tools from one stone. This suggests that their knapping techniques were more evolved.

BACK TO YOUR ROOTS

Maybe you stumbled upon a handaxe-shaped rock when you were a kid and tried cutting something with it. Congratulations, you've been using handaxes without even realizing it. Maybe it's in your DNA.

If you're looking for a fun activity to connect with our early ancestors, go down to a river and find a river rock to craft your very own stone handaxe. After you've found your axe stone, find another harder stone or "hammerstone" that you can use to shape your handaxe. Use the hammerstone to strike flakes off the handaxe until it's teardrop shaped. Once you've finished chiseling and shaping your handaxe, you can sand it down by looking for a large flat rock surface. Put some sand on the rock surface and pour some water on it. Now press your handaxe onto the surface and glide it across, maintaining pressure to make sure it's keeping enough contact to sand off some material. Focus your sanding on the edge to make it more narrow. Repeat this until you're happy with its look and feel (or until you're too tired and hungry to keep going). Now you've just made yourself a stone handaxe! Your *Homo erectus* ancestors would be proud.

Celt

The celt (pronounced "selt" and not "kelt," which refers to a Celtic person) is another notable stone axe tool used during the Neolithic period. A celt may look like a long, thin stone with a narrow edge that may be attached to a shaft of wood for a handle. Some celts had a groove around the stone closer to the back end. With that additional groove, the celt could wedge into a piece of wood for a handle and the groove would help it stay in place. The celt could also be fashioned to the wood with fibers and string to tie it in place. Once the wooden handle was introduced to the axe, it's striking power was amplified. The addition of the handle helped protect the user's hands and allowed them to expend less energy by giving the axe extra momentum. Many different parts of the world had their own style of celt; some ancient celts were more triangle-shaped and some more rectangular. Some could weigh over 20 pounds (9 kg) and some were very light. It is generally thought that the celt was used for chopping and cutting wood, but it could also have been used for hunting and other tasks. Eventually, these tools were made from copper and iron and were traded across the world.

Labrys

The double-axe, also known historically as a labrys, was made famous in the Bronze Age by the Minoan civilization of Crete (c. 2700–1450 BCE). For the Minoans, the labrys was more than a utility tool; it seemed to have a lot of symbolic and spiritual significance. It is believed that the Minoans invented the labrys. The word *labyrinth* might also come from Minoan origins, meaning "palace of the double-axe." A labyrinth is a very complex and confusing maze. According to ancient myths, the labyrinth at the Palace of Knossos in Crete imprisoned the Minotaur, a dreaded monster with the head of a bull and the body of a man. Throughout studies of Minoan culture, you'll come across the labrys on pottery and in carvings, including very elegantly designed labrys you wouldn't trust yourself with on a backcountry camping trip. This is an example of when a tool becomes more than just a thing you use, but also something with spiritual and cultural significance.

Battle Axe

I've found most people seem to associate axes with two groups if you ask them for an immediate mental image: the logger, with a felling axe, and the Viking, with a battle axe. Battle axes can indeed be traced back to the Vikings. Naturally, battle axes were designed to be well balanced and light so they could be easily carried. Some had shorter wood shafts, which made them easier to hide and use with one hand, and others were made with longer shafts for various fighting techniques, such as trying to swing at someone's head with great momentum from a distance. The longer axes also required two hands to use efficiently.

> **FACT**
> In Sweden, axes were the preferred tool for executions in the eighteenth and nineteenth centuries, with the last usage being in 1910.

Some axes were designed with "beards," a blade that extends lower than a traditional axe, making it possible to hook the axe onto things like shields and body parts.

Tomahawk

Okay, I said there were two main mental images people think of in the last section, but there is a possible third. Depending on where you live, there's a chance the first axe you think of is a tomahawk axe, which is most closely associated with certain Indigenous peoples in North America. It is currently believed that the tomahawk was first created by the Algonquin Native Americans. This makes sense because the word *tomahawk* was derived from the Algonquian word *otomahuk*, *tomahak*, or *tomahakan*, meaning "used for cutting" or "to cut down."

One of the most distinct versions of the tomahawk resembles a hatchet, but tomahawks can also have a unique modification: opposite the blade, the axe may sport a "tomahawk poll," which could be a spike, a hammer, or a pipe.

Tomahawk is also used in okichitaw, an Indigenous martial art, where people are trained to use and defend against this weapon. Some of the training may include throwing, hooking with the blade, striking, and precision swinging, among other attacks.

In the 1600s, the trades between Indigenous peoples and European settlers brought new materials and forging techniques to tomahawk axe construction. When new metal-blade tomahawks were introduced, they became a valuable trading commodity. But even after European settlers and Indigenous peoples began trading, that didn't mean stone axes vanished.

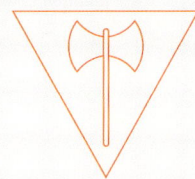

THE EMPOWERMENT OF LABRYS

For the Minoans, it is thought that the labrys was a sacred symbol used by women to worship the Mother Goddess and was potentially used for bull sacrifice rituals conducted by priestesses.

For the mythical and ancient nation of women warriors of the Amazon, the double-axe had a different purpose and became a notable fighting weapon. The women of the Amazon were legendary in their battle skills. They were often depicted on horseback with badass biceps and as many weapons as they could carry. You probably wouldn't want to get in the path of an Amazon woman swinging a labrys.

While the purpose of the axe between the two cultures was different, the female empowerment behind the axe held strong. This symbolism eventually led the labrys to become a symbol for female empowerment in the twentieth century and a symbol for lesbianism in the 1970s. The labrys was also put on a rendition of the lesbian flag, created in 1999 and published in the *Gay and Lesbian Times* newspaper in June 2000. The flag features a lavender background with an inverted black triangle, a reclaimed symbol once used by the Nazis to label gay people. At the center of the triangle is a labrys, representing the strength, resilience, and empowerment of women.

In 2004 a group of lesbians, bisexuals, transgender, and allies formed in Kyrgyzstan with the mission to protect people's rights and empower the LGBTQ communities of Kyrgyzstan. They called their group Labrys.

THE CONNECTION TO YOUR TOOL

The relationship between Indigenous peoples and their tools held more significance than most colonial views of tools. The way many Indigenous peoples look at what we might call "objects," such as rocks and pieces of wood, has deeper meaning stemming from their language and beliefs. Many Indigenous beliefs teach that everything has a spirit. The rock that has been carved into the shape of a handaxe is more than an inanimate object; it's a being that has been transformed into something with another purpose and that being should be respected and honored. Even in many Indigenous languages, words tend to be more verb-centric, where objects are described with motion and as beings. In contrast, many colonial languages are noun-centric, where objects are described as inanimate. The Indigenous perspective also highlights the collaboration humans have with nature when making and using these tools.

An axe is an extension of one's inner strength and skill.

Forged by fire, crafted with purpose, and built for power.

SHAPING
NORTH AMERICA

In the early 1700s, steel was introduced into the axe-making process. Steel is harder and stronger than iron and holds a sharp edge, so this was a major improvement. Around the time of the Industrial Revolution, axes started being mass produced and were cast by various companies, especially in North America. These axes became a driving force that shaped the North American landscape in the late 1600s through the 1900s.

There was another important change during this time period: Axes began to grow in size as the need for felling trees to clear land became a primary task for developing communities. The handles of the axe became longer and heavier so the person using the axe didn't have to rely so much on their own power and could allow the tool to do more of the work. Increasingly narrow and stretched-out blades also began to appear, which helped with a variety of logging tasks and the building of log homes.

EVEN MORE AXE STYLES

Many cultures had their own spin on the axe, and as trading became possible it brought more influence, designs, and ideas to the axe's evolution. With the invention of chainsaws, you might think innovation would have died for axes. That is not the case. I'm convinced the axe will never go out of use. There have been many new styles and designs of axes introduced over the years. Some of the popular ones in North America include the felling axe, the double bit, the Pulaski, the hatchet, the Hudson Bay, and the splitting maul, to name a few.

Some axe heads have very wide, heavy wedges, and others have thin, narrow blades. Many trades have their own preferred axes. In this section, I'll cover a few of the more common specialty axes you may come across today.

Each axe tells its own story of grit, tradition, and timeless strength.

ANTIQUE AXES

Whenever I travel, I have a habit of stopping at local antique shops. They offer a glimpse into the region's history through its treasures. Naturally, I'm always drawn to the section with old tools, often tucked away in a back corner. Through my antique store adventures, I've discovered many unique axe styles—some unfamiliar, as they've been reshaped by their previous owners or maybe crafted for a specific purpose.

A tip for looking at old axes is to try and find any markers on the metal that could indicate where and by whom the axe was originally made. Sometimes the metal will be so worn down that the markers have faded, but the shape of the axe head is also an indicator. During the mass production of axes, some companies had signature axe head shapes, also called "patterns." The shape of the axe head can help narrow down the region where the axe was created. For instance, in the American northwest, there are more softwoods that can be felled and chopped with a broad and narrow axe head. In the east there are more hardwoods, which need a wider axe head in order to chop into the denser wood. The density, size, and difficulty of the region's wood influences the shape of their woodchopping axes.

Bushcraft Hatchet:

A hatchet is a smaller, lighter, and more versatile axe and is usually used as a single hand tool for various tasks like chopping kindling. It is similar to a carving axe, but a carving axe has a very specific bevel used for more precision slicing, while a bushcraft hatchet is made for chopping and tasks you might be doing while you're camping or backcountry hiking (hopefully that task doesn't include throwing it at something that might want to eat you).

Carving Axe:

Built with a short handle with a sharp, narrow blade, this little axe is primarily used for precision carving and craftsmanship woodworking. Unlike a splitting maul, the user of a carving axe isn't going to want to do a whole lot of power swinging, more like calculated slicing. This is a handy little tool when you have a really beautiful piece of wood you want to carve down in order to make a nifty wood spoon.

Racing Axe:

Also known as a competition axe, this axe is used at logging sport events. It is lightweight with a thin blade and a sharp edge. The design gives it the advantage of agility and speed. Some of the competitions you'll see these axes in are underhand chopping, standing block chopping, and springboard chopping.

Felling Axe:

This is a classic forestry axe with a long handle and a wide, narrow head and usually weighs 2 to 4 pounds (1 to 2 kg). It is designed to cut across the tree and remove a wedge shape that will make the tree fall over. The long handle helps the user gain momentum to allow the wide and narrow head to cut into the grain of the tree. Chainsaws have replaced a lot of these axe-based methods of felling a tree, but the felling axe is still a great wood chopping tool to have around.

Tomahawk:

Deserving another mention, this axe has played many significant roles, including being a tool, a weapon, and a symbol for war and peace, with the blade representing war while the blunt side is sometimes crafted as a pipe that could be used to smoke tobacco, a sacred and significant plant for many Native American cultures. These axes are a great utility tool for chopping small campfire wood, and they're really fun to throw.

Double Blade:

There are many styles and patterns within the double-bladed axe category. The two blades assist each other with cutting the work in half (pun intended). One blade can be kept sharp for splitting rounds of wood and the other blade left a little more dull for chopping off branches and obstructions in the tree.

Fire Axe:

Probably the only axe you'll see in almost every building in an urban city, the fire axe is a great thing to have in emergencies. Commonly, a fire axe will be colored red and have a head with a blade on one end and a pick on the other. This gives you options for when you or a first responder might need to break down doors, smash open windows, break holes in walls, or open the roof for ventilation in a fire. This axe might be one of the coolest, but let's hope you'll never have to swing it.

Hudson Bay:

Along with the tomahawk, this was another notable trading axe during the time of the fur trade in North America and was built by French traders who were working along the Hudson Bay route. The head typically weighs around 2 pounds (910 g) and is used for light chopping. This axe can also be a great companion for backcountry camping or as a utility axe.

Broad Axe:

As the name suggests, this axe has a very broad head with the functions of timber framing for log homes, shipbuilding, and forming railroad ties. Along with the broad head comes a bit more weight and a longer handle to help the user make an impactful strike in the wood without a lot of force.

Splitting Maul:

This axe is a powerhouse! Designed with a heavy, wide wedge and long handle, this axe is used for splitting big wood rounds or tackling knots in wood. It's a pretty hefty tool for hefty jobs, which means it's not going to be your go-to axe, but you'll appreciate having it in your shed when you come across some of those "unsplittable" pieces. Use of this axe can take practice to really be able to master. With the longer handle and the heavier head, it can be a bit harder to control.

Tactical Axe:

An axe used for fighting, the tactical axe is made to be light, balanced, and with a very sharp edge. It usually has a rubber or fiberglass handle to keep it from breaking. Sometimes the axe head has pieces carved out to get rid of any unnecessary metal and make the axe lighter. Some militaries and martial artists train to fight and defend with these axes.

Pickaxe:

This axe has a T-shaped head with one side having a long, sharp pick edge and the other side having a wide, flat shape. These tools are for breaking rocks and hard ground and are used in mining. They can be a really handy landscaping tool for people living in rocky areas.

ANATOMY OF AN AXE

In its simplest form, an axe is a metal blade attached to a handle. But in order to better understand, use, and eventually fix an axe, it helps to get to know the anatomy and terminology.

A. Bit/Blade: The sharp edge of the axe that makes contact to cut. Some axes have double bits and some bits need to be extra sharp for precise cutting. Some bits have more of a curve and others are flat with a bevel. The utility of the axe will determine the shape and sharpness of the bit.

B. Toe: The upper corner of the bit.

C. Heel: The lower corner of the bit. Typically, the heel is the first point of contact for wood chopping.

D. Poll/Butt: The back end of the axe head. It is usually flat or can be slightly rounded. On some axes, you can use the poll as a hammer or use a hammer to pound the axe head into a wood piece to split it.

E. Eye: The hole in the axe head where the handle is fitted. Typically, it will be in the shape of a teardrop. Different axes will have differently shaped eyes, which is good to be aware of when you're rehandling an axe.

F. Shoulder: Near the top of the handle where the metal head and wood meet. The shoulder is usually shaped a bit thicker than the middle of the handle, as it sometimes takes a bit of impact while chopping wood. You can also get leather wraps to protect your axe's shoulder to keep it from breaking.

G. Belly: The longest part of the handle that provides a path for your hands to move while chopping.

H. Throat: On some axes, this area has a slight curve to help your hands know their position on the handle.

I. Knob: The very end of your axe. It is usually in a deer-foot shape to add a bit of thickness to the end of your handle to keep your hands from slipping too far.

J. Cheek: The side of the axe. The thickness of the cheek or the presence of extra bevels in the cheek can affect the way the axe splits the wood.

Let's say you have some fresh rounds of big leaf maple. Would you choose a single hand bushcraft hatchet or a wide wedge splitting maul to chop through that dense hardwood? I'm sure you could do it with a hatchet, but it might take you until next winter. Choosing the right axe for the job can save you time and energy and lower the potential for frustration—trust me.

Generally speaking, when you're chopping bigger, denser pieces of wood, you're going to want a wider, heavier axe. But a bigger axe doesn't always mean it's more efficient for the job.

I can say from experience that, although an 8-pound (7 kg) splitting maul can split most woods, I wouldn't use it every time I go out to chop. Why? Because I'd be wasting a lot of energy wielding that extra weight when some more precise chops with a lighter axe in the right areas of the wood can do the same job and save my energy. In such a case, you must also consider the element of accuracy over power. When you're able to read the wood grain to determine the best place for your blade to strike, you won't need as many big heavy swings to break apart the wood fiber. We'll explore more about how to read the wood in chapter 2. Even though a heavier axe will give you weight to wield, a heavier axe will also yield less precision with your swing. However, with a lighter axe, you can have more control, but it might not give you the force you need. In the end, it's a balance of knowing what weight you're able to wield with control and confidence and what weight will be able to split the wood. Wood-chopping practice and wood knowledge are the best ways to assess your

approach. Don't worry if you're new to all this; we'll get you swinging with confidence in no time.

Another way to help you find a good axe length is by comparing it with your arm length. Pick an axe and grip it just below the head where the metal meets the handle. Bring your arm straight out to your side at shoulder height, then bring the knob of the axe in line with your arm. If the knob goes past your shoulder to your chest, the axe may be too big to start with. Find an axe length where the base of the head and the knob are around the same length as your arm. You'll have a better chance of controlling the swing with that length.

CHOOSING AN AXE FOR WOODCHOPPING

When choosing your axe, first ask yourself, *What am I chopping?* Are you after freshly cut rounds of knotted hardwood that you're going to stack and store for next winter? Or are you chopping up some dry, smaller pieces of softwood that will be thrown straight into a campfire? These questions will help you narrow down the length, design, and weight of your chosen axe.

Which Handle Can Handle It?

A common debate in the woodchopping axe world is which material works best for a handle. As you start searching for axes to add to your collection, you're going to come across axes with rubber, plastic, and fiberglass handles. There are pros and cons to those materials. Some of the bonuses are that they are more durable than wood handles and easier to maintain. They can also be lighter than wood handles, so they're great for begin-

SPLITTING WEDGE (A GOOD OL' SIDEKICK)

Another tool that can be a great sidekick to an axe when tackling a load for firewood is a splitting wedge. Place the narrow end of the wedge on the wood in the area most likely to split and hammer it down. Keep pounding until it pushes the wood open.

You can occasionally use the butt of a single-bit axe as a sledge-hammer to pound in the wedge. It's common to do this with a heavy axe, like a splitting maul, but not all butts are meant to be hammers. Make sure your axe is designed with a solid butt or use a sledgehammer with the wedge instead.

One advantage of using a wedge is that it allows you to focus your force on a specific point in the wood, rather than trying to hit the exact spot with your blade. This lets you concentrate your energy more effectively. Wedges are a lot wider than most axe heads, so it really helps to push the knotty and dense wood apart where a narrow head axe might get stuck (refer to chapter 2 on how to get a stuck axe out of wood).

ners. Personally, I prefer wood handles, but if someone is completely new to woodchopping, I'm going to recommend that they get an axe with a fiberglass handle. An axe with a fiberglass handle is lightweight, less likely to break, and the material absorbs shock pretty well. Plus, it's pretty common to come across in most hardware stores.

But, if these other materials are so great, why is everyone so into wood handles? Wood handles in North America are commonly made from hickory or ash. These woods are very dense and can withstand a lot of punishment. They also have great shock absorption, which is a bonus, though some fiberglass handles are also on the same level of shock absorption. Again, why wood? For most people, it's the feel of the handle. Maybe some of it is nostalgia or sentimentality, but there is something special about wood handles. As I said before, I personally prefer wood handles for many reasons. Yes, they are more likely to break, but a broken handle brings an opportunity to upcycle an axe, which is an empowering task that every woodchopper should try at least once (we'll discuss how to rehandle an axe in chapter 3). A wood handle brings you deeper into the experience of woodchopping. As we explored earlier, using a blade attached to a solid wood handle is how we humans have been chopping for thousands of years.

Wood or fiberglass: one rooted in tradition, the other built for modern resilience. The choice is yours.

TRAITS AND CHARACTERISTICS OF AXE HANDLES

PLASTIC, RUBBER, AND FIBERGLASS HANDLES

✓ They are very durable and low maintenance.

✓ Some of these handles can have a better grip.

✓ They can be lighter than wood

✓ There are a lot of interesting textures, colors, and designs.

WOOD HANDLES

✓ When they break, you can rehandle them.

✓ You can carve grip lines in the areas where you need more grip.

✓ They have great shock absorption.

✓ Some wood handles have curves to aid in hand placement with your swing.

In the end, the choice of axe ultimately comes down to you. What feels good in your hands? What helps you swing with control and chop with confidence? It's important to find an axe that is right for you.

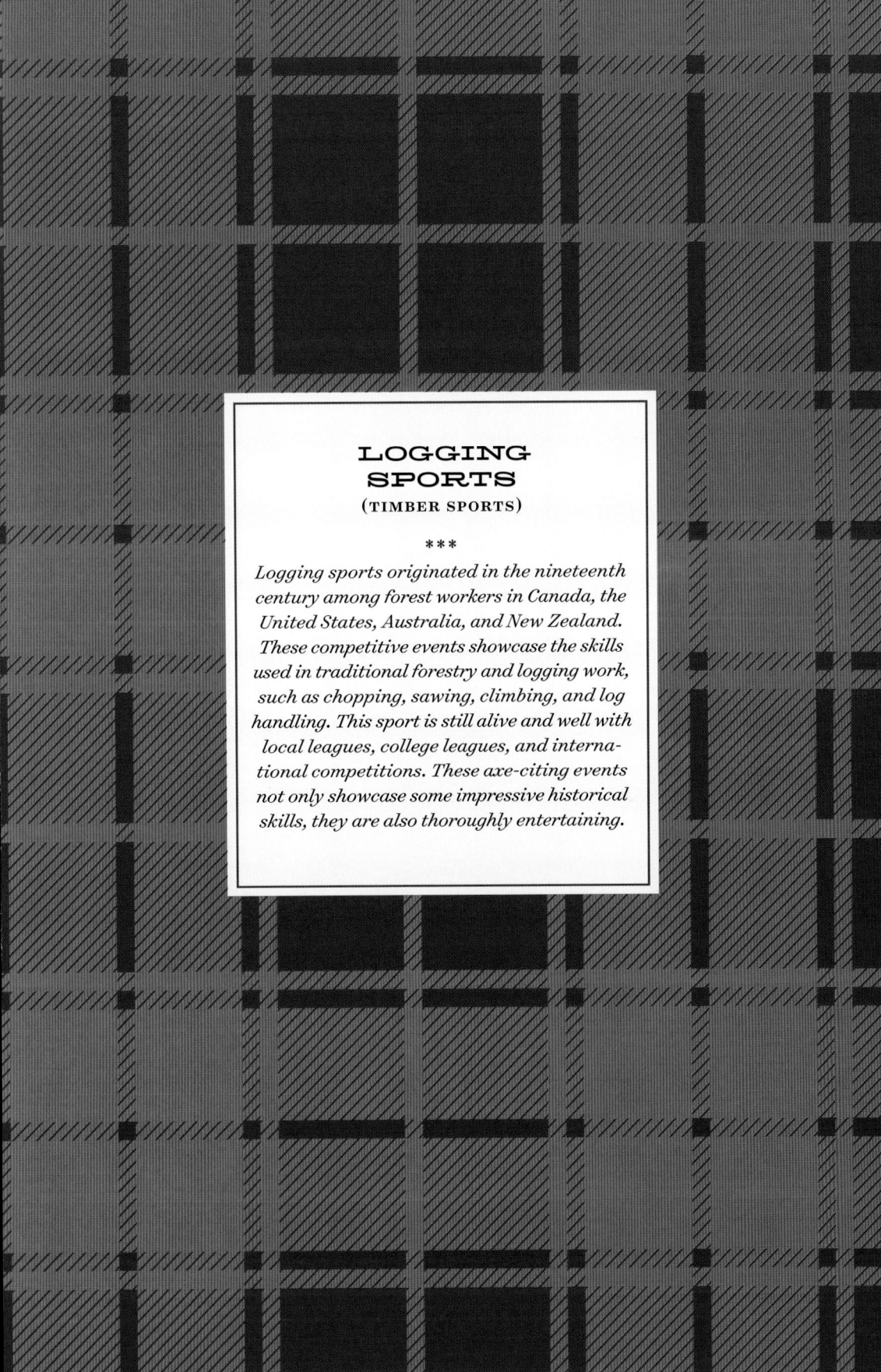

LOGGING SPORTS
(TIMBER SPORTS)

***

Logging sports originated in the nineteenth century among forest workers in Canada, the United States, Australia, and New Zealand. These competitive events showcase the skills used in traditional forestry and logging work, such as chopping, sawing, climbing, and log handling. This sport is still alive and well with local leagues, college leagues, and international competitions. These axe-citing events not only showcase some impressive historical skills, they are also thoroughly entertaining.

CHAPTER 2

CHOPPING WOOD

Before we swing into things, I want to ask why you picked up this book. I'm going to guess it's for one of two reasons: either you've had a lot of experience chopping firewood and are familiar with the process of using wood as heat or you are new to woodchopping and curious about this skill and method of self-sufficiency. Whether you are an experienced chopper or just starting your woodchopping journey, this chapter will help you set up the most pragmatic woodchopping environment, help you tune up your axe swing for efficiency, and add some age-old tips and tricks to the process, including how to read the wood to find the best spots to hit for splitting.

Most of these points come from personal experience and wisdom from a small island town woodchopping group called the Green Angels Wood Choppers. This group is primarily made up of retired men, me, and some drop-in choppers. The group sources local trees, fells the trees (cuts them down), limbs the trees (removes the branches), bucks the wood (cuts a tree into usable lengths, usually with a chainsaw), and then chops the wood into firewood. The wood is then sold to people in the community and the revenue is donated to various community initiatives. In the group, there are people from all walks of life. Some people in the group have lived in urban areas most of their lives and came into woodchopping very recently, and some have been chopping most of their life. One of the best parts of this group and other similar community woodchopping groups is that everyone is willing to learn from each other and teach each other. It's a humbling skill that involves connecting with nature and community.

Woodchopping is something humans have been doing for thousands of years. It's something we've passed down from generation to generation. Different regions of the world have their own twists on this skill adapted to their environment. Slowly, new methods have been added as we learn more and adapt old approaches.

Building skills and community

Plus, new technologies have evolved woodchopping entirely. The hydraulic wood splitter was revolutionary for people who use wood as heat. This technology came out in the late 1950s. Hydraulic wood splitters use hydraulic pressure to drive a wedge into the wood to split it along the grain. This technology increases the speed and ease of splitting wood, which makes it more accessible to people who have time and energy limitations for human-powered woodchopping.

But the experience of learning and teaching the age-old skill of chopping wood will always be something that brings people together. So, let's learn and get chopping!

GETTING READY TO CHOP

The atmosphere of a woodchopping environment is often characterized by the sounds of splitting wood, the scent of freshly cut timber, the aesthetics of wood pieces stacked up to dry, and the tactile experience of handling an axe. The choice of environment can impact the efficiency, safety, and overall experience of chopping wood. So first, let's talk about the woodchopping environment setup.

The Chopping Environment

This environment can vary widely and includes factors such as the location, whether it's in a rural backyard, a wooded area, or an indoor space with proper ventilation.

For an efficient setup, let's start from the ground up. You want to find an even, solid area with good drainage. Chopping on soft, mushy ground will absorb the force of the axe and make it more difficult to split your wood pieces. Sometimes,

Start with clean, even ground to build a good foundation for your chopping setup.

if the ground is extra soft, it will cause your wood to bounce from the impact of your axe's swing. Don't get me wrong, trying to chop bouncing wood can be a fun game and force you to get better at your axe accuracy, but be forewarned that the game loses its fun really fast. So avoid bouncy wood frustration and keep everything solid for efficiency. It's also more likely that soft ground will turn to muddy ground, and we want to make sure we keep our wood dry and healthy for burning. So to emphasize yet again, set up your chopping environment on solid earth with good drainage.

The Chopping Block

Now that we've covered the ground, let's move up to the heart of every chopping environment—the chopping block. A chopping block is typically a larger round of wood that you will be using as a platform for chopping other wood pieces. The block's job is to be a solid platform for you to place your wood pieces on and to give your axe a good height and target to make the split.

The chopping block might seem like such a simple element in your chopping setup, but it will really make or break the flow of your chopping sessions. Its primary role lies in providing a stable and elevated surface for splitting logs into manageable pieces and ensuring safety and efficiency by preventing the axe from striking the ground and damaging the blade. You want to put a bit more intention into choosing your block than just choosing any random round. Find a wood round that sits flat on the ground and will be wider than any other wood you might be chopping.

We know we want to keep the chopping block wide, but what about height? You don't want your block to be too high, as it will prevent you from having a full

Solid ground with a sturdy chopping block will make your chopping time a great time.

follow-through with your axe. Something higher than your waist will be considered too high. But as usual, there are exceptions. If you're chopping only kindling and small pieces that won't need full axe force, then you might want a higher block to make it more comfortable for processing smaller wood pieces. For a multipurpose chopping block, find a round that measures below your knees so it will allow you to have a very thorough swing for medium pieces, while also being ergonomically friendly for kindling. A general rule for finding the height of your chopping block is: the smaller the pieces you want to chop, the higher your chopping block can be while still allowing you to swing a hatchet. For chopping bigger pieces, you want to have a chopping platform that is very low to the ground to allow for the full follow-through of your axe. Sometimes it's good to have at least two chopping blocks of different heights—one high block for smaller wood pieces and one lower block for medium to large wood pieces.

Once again, I'm going to emphasize that your chopping block needs to be solid and stable for it to be efficient. To test the capability of your block and stability of the ground it's on, you can hit it with a sledgehammer or the butt of an axe to make sure it can absorb the impact without moving.

Once you've found your block and a good piece of ground to place it on, check overhead and a few feet in each direction. Make sure you have a clear path above you for your axe to freely swing. Look out for any branches or obstacles from above. Sometimes you'll get some free-radical wood pieces that fly off in different directions from a chop. Double-check that your chopping block is at a good distance from anything that could be hit with rogue wood pieces. Scan above you and all around you to make sure the area is safely spaced out.

Once you have your chopping area ready, let's get chopping!

CHOPPING THE WOOD

Now that we have our environment ready, let's grab our axe (we've explored choosing the right axe for you in chapter 1), and let's get swinging! We'll break down the proper chopping techniques into three steps:

Step 1: Your Distance

1. Place your wood piece on the chopping block so that it sits very solidly on the platform.

2. Measure the distance between you and the wood piece with your axe by setting the blade where you want it to land and stand holding your hands near the knob of the axe in the position they will be in at the end of your swing.

Start by putting the axe where you want it to land and then get it there with as much force and control as you can.

Step 2: Your Stance

1. Now that you're at the right distance, it's time to get into the chopping stance. Start with your feet shoulder-width apart and a slight bend in your knees.

2. Hold your dominant hand by the axe's head and your other hand near the knob (end) of the handle.

FACT

If you find you're missing your target, it's likely you're overreaching. When the axe is coming down, your arms may tend to stretch forward. If this is happening, try taking half a step backward. It just might do the trick.

Step 3: Chopping

1. Raise your axe straight up overhead as far back as you can while keeping it straight.

2. Propel the axe forward with your dominant hand and guide it down. Remember not to force it down but let it fall while keeping it in line with your target. As it comes down, your dominant hand slides down to the end to meet the other hand that is stationed at the knob.

3. As the axe comes down, lower into a slight squat to allow the axe a full follow-through.

The three steps just listed are the basic chopping mechanics, but in order to get your axe to cut into the wood, the movements have to be fluid to harness some force and momentum. This is where repetition and practice come in. The more comfortable you get with the motions of the swing, the better your swing will become.

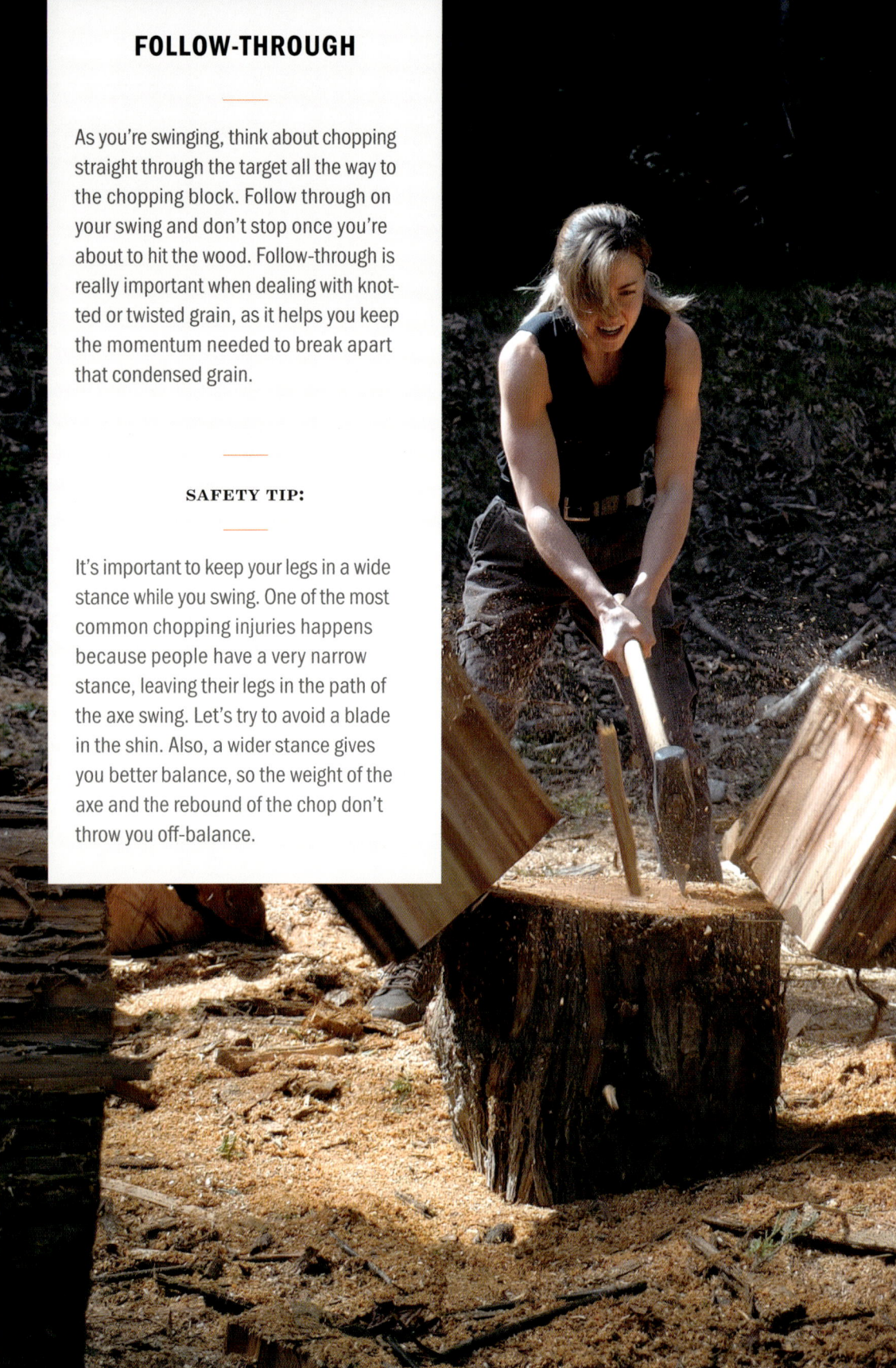

FOLLOW-THROUGH

As you're swinging, think about chopping straight through the target all the way to the chopping block. Follow through on your swing and don't stop once you're about to hit the wood. Follow-through is really important when dealing with knotted or twisted grain, as it helps you keep the momentum needed to break apart that condensed grain.

SAFETY TIP:

It's important to keep your legs in a wide stance while you swing. One of the most common chopping injuries happens because people have a very narrow stance, leaving their legs in the path of the axe swing. Let's try to avoid a blade in the shin. Also, a wider stance gives you better balance, so the weight of the axe and the rebound of the chop don't throw you off-balance.

Power Up! Take Your Chopping to New Levels

Woodchopping is a primal, practical, and powerful activity. Each swing of the axe requires physical strength and technical skills to split wood effectively. It's an activity that not only rewards your efforts in the short-term—from the instant satisfaction of hearing the axe crack through the wood and seeing it fall to pieces—but it is also a gift that keeps on giving. As you go out to your pile to bring firewood inside to heat up your woodstove, you'll continuously thank your past self for all your efforts. The sweat and labor from one season can help you stay warm and cozy through a frigid winter.

"The Flick"

Make sure you use the blade of your axe and really get a cut into the wood as you chop. This is achieved by "the flick." Instead of hammering straight down with the blade, you want to create a slight sweeping motion as the blade hits the wood. This is achieved by a subtle but quick movement of your wrists. In your swing, as the axe is coming down, just as the blade touches the wood, cock your wrist upward so the blade "flicks" and swipes the wood instead of hammers it. It's very subtle, but you'll feel it when you get it.

DOES SIZE MATTER?

The type of wood you're chopping influences the size and style of axe you need. But bigger is not always better or necessary. The size of the axe you need for chopping wood depends on various factors, including the type and size of wood you'll be chopping, your physical strength, and your personal preferences. If you aren't comfortable swinging an 8-pound (4 kg) splitting maul to chop some 22-inch (56 cm) rounds, you don't need to. The most important thing is to feel comfortable with your tool. With proper techniques, you can chop big and difficult pieces with smaller axes. While a bigger axe or splitting maul can provide more splitting force for larger logs, the choice ultimately depends on your specific needs and physical capabilities. It's a good idea to have a variety of axes or tools on hand for different tasks, including a smaller axe or hatchet for more detailed work and a larger one for heavy-duty splitting.

Build Your Power Swing

Now that you're a pro at chopping, let's amp up the power behind your swing. Using the same swing motion and mechanics, we're going to add a few more muscles to the mix.

Get the hips and glutes involved:

In your starting position, get a bit lower into that squat. When you're ready to swing, initiate the movement by squeezing your glutes to get your hip to thrust forward, using that momentum to raise your axe overhead. As your axe is coming back down, squat down with the downward motion of the axe.

Get onto your toes:

Sometimes, an extra inch can go a long way, so let's add some heightening foot-work. Starting with your feet solidly on the ground, as you initiate your swing and hoist your axe overhead, come onto your toes for some extra height. Then as the axe comes down, plant firmly onto your heels and keep going into your squat.

Remember to breathe. Inhale as you raise your axe and exhale as it comes down.

HOW TO READ WOOD

It's important to read the wood to assess its characteristics and condition before chopping. This involves understanding the grain pattern, identifying knots, checking for cracks or irregularities, and gauging the overall quality of the wood.

Examining the grain helps determine the natural lines along which the wood is more likely to split cleanly. Identifying knots is crucial because they can be tougher to chop through and may affect the predictability of the split. Checking for cracks or other imperfections ensures that the wood is solid and won't pose unexpected challenges during the chopping process. Being able to read the wood helps you identify the challenges on a wood piece to mentally prepare for the challenge before your axe hits the wood and you physically feel it.

Learning to read the wood was a game changer for me. In my early years of woodchopping, I spent a lot of time just blindly swinging an axe into wood with as much force as possible. Although blind forceful swinging can work, it isn't always effective, and you'll lose energy quickly. When I started to take a quick overview of each piece of wood to assess its potential weak areas and challenges it really made my swings count and sped up the process.

Some tree cut provides a clear map for your axe.

Wood can form cracks—not just from drying out but also from internal stress. Same with humans: too much internal stress and we'll crack as well.

Follow the Rays

When you're ready to swing your axe and split some wood, find the path of least resistance in the grain to really make your swings count. You're going to look for a few hints that'll lead you to find the wood's sweet spot. Take a look at the grain to see whether there are already any cracks or openings in the wood. Usually in dry wood you'll see some cracks, also known as rays. These indicate that the moisture is leaving the wood and they provide a good target for your swing. If you're able to hit one of these cracks with your blade, the wood will be more likely to open. But when you're splitting freshly felled wood or "wet wood" you probably won't have these rays due to the moisture content of the wood.

FACT

According to a Harvard study, woodchopping can burn over 250 calories per 30 minutes of chopping. As they say, "Firewood heats you twice." Who needs a gym membership when you've got a pile of wood to chop?

Knots can become nails that keep the wood together. They will also cause your axe head to get caught in the irregular and dense grain.

How Not to Knot

Chopping through a knot in wood can be a challenging task due to the dense and often twisted nature of the wood fibers in that area. Knots are sections where branches or limbs once grew, resulting in a concentration of tightly packed wood cells. These knotted pieces don't usually look pretty, but they sure do make great night logs.

When you're tackling a piece of wood with a knot, try not to aim right for that mass of condensed wood, unless you enjoy being in a state of frustration. Knotted wood can really test your patience and tolerance for frustration. But knotted pieces can make great firewood because the extra mass of the knot makes the wood burn longer. So,

when you're tackling a knot, avoid trying to chop across the path of the knot; instead, try skimming it. Chop away as much of the wood beside the knot to break the bond and loosen the wood around it.

Another thing to keep in mind and add to your frustration is that your axe will be more likely to get stuck if you're chopping close to a knot. This is because the wood around the knot is likely more dense and twisted. To keep your axe head from getting stuck, try using an axe with a wider head, such as a splitting maul, or this would be a good time to bring out a splitting wedge. If you're using a splitting wedge, place it beside the knot to break away the surrounding wood.

Chopping Patterns

When you've got a big 22-inch (56 cm) round in front of you, it can seem daunting to think about how to break it down into stackable pieces. Let's explore two options to get the splits going.

You can try a center split by having your swings create a line through the center of the wood and keep chopping that line until the wood splits in two. This approach takes a lot of initial energy and power to make that initial split, but the flowing chops will become easier and easier as the pieces get smaller. Alternatively, you can start from the outside and work your way in. Start your swings closer to the bark/outside of the wood. This area is going to be softer and easier to chop pieces off of. Start chopping the outside and work your way to the center. This approach requires more consistent energy and is usually the preferred method for big rounds. However, the initial center split does look the coolest, so you can choose between stylish and practical.

Chopping through the center will require more power up front. Chopping along the outer wood will need more constant power throughout the chop, but it might take a bit longer.

STUCK AXE?

Is your axe getting stuck in the wood? There are few reasons why this might happen.

The first reason might be your axe head. If you're trying to chop big rounds that have a tight grain while using an axe with a narrow head, it's not going to work so well. You want to use an axe with a wide head, such as a splitting maul, to help push apart the wood as you chop. A general rule of thumb is that light, narrow-headed axes are great for small chops and small pieces, while bigger rounds require bigger axe heads.

But let's say you're using a bushcraft axe to chop some smaller rounds and it seems to be getting stuck in the grain even though it's the right axe for the job. Time to bring in some assistance. Using some WD-40 or any type of oil or lubricant on the axe head will smooth the chopping and prevent the blade from getting stuck.

Sometimes, the weather also affects the potential for the axe to get stuck. When wood is exposed to cold temperatures, it contracts. Conversely, when it is exposed to heat, it expands. This is called thermal expansion. If you're trying to chop some freshly felled wood on a cooler day, it might be more reluctant to open up. But let's throw in another scenario. What about if the wood is frozen? That might actually be easier. When the wood has been left out in freezing temperatures, the fibers in the wood are compromised and not held together as tightly. This makes it easier for the wood to split open with fewer chops. The downside of chopping frozen wood is the ice factor. You might need to chop through a few layers of ice before getting to the wood.

When the axe is stuck, either loosen it from the wood or use the locked axe to your advantage.

Chopping Wet vs. Dry

When it comes to chopping, it's easier to chop through dry wood than wet wood. Wet wood contains a higher moisture content, making it denser and more challenging to split. The excess water can make the fibers more flexible, reducing the effectiveness of each strike. Chopping wet wood requires more physical effort because the moisture makes it less likely for the axe to bite into the wood. There is also a risk of the axe bouncing back. Wet wood has a greater tendency to absorb the impact of the axe and requires more physical effort. Wet wood can be messy and stress-inducing to chop, but sometimes we can't be too picky about the wood we have access to and, at the end of the day, if the wood will burn, you'll probably use it.

If you want to spend some time chopping wet wood into woodstove size pieces, the smaller size will help the wood dry faster and will be more convenient for storing.

There are a lot of signs of wood seasoning, from weight to changes in the grain to color.

Chopping kindling

Chopping small pieces of kindling will require a different approach than how we split large rounds of wood. Would a wide, 8-pound splitting maul be an ideal axe to chop thin pieces of kindling? Not really—trust me, I have tried it. Smaller pieces of wood mean using a smaller, more precise axe like a 12-inch (30 cm) hatchet.

When chopping kindling pieces, aim for a thickness of 1 to 2 inches (2.5 to 5 cm)—but vary this depending on your needs. Because some people chop kindling by holding a block of wood at one end and swinging the axe at the other to slice off pieces, it can lead to some close calls with the blade and your fingers. Let's take a look at some other methods.

Wood hold:

Instead of using your hand to hold onto the wood pieces you're chopping, use another piece of wood to hold the chopping piece in place.

You want to cut kindling close to the thickness of a finger, but you don't want to cut off a finger in the process.

Batoning:

Place the blade on the wood piece and use another piece of wood to strike the back of the blade, driving it through the wood.

Contact chop:

Place the knob of your hatchet and blade on the wood piece you want to split. Grip the knob of your axe to the wood piece with both hands around the axe and wood. Raise it up slightly and tap it down on the chopping block so the blade bites into the wood to keep it in place. Then, raise it up higher and bring it all down with more force for the axe to split the wood.

Using kindling allows for a controlled and gradual start to a fire, which can improve the overall burn quality and reduce the amount of smoke produced.

WOODSY
WORKOUT

***

Chopping wood is a great stress release,
a practical chore, and a really great workout.
Depending on the intensity, you can burn
between 400 to 600 calories per hour while
chopping wood. It's an activity that combines
strength, focus, endurance, and cardio.
As they say, firewood heats you twice: once
while chopping, then while burning.

CHAPTER 3

HANG YOUR AXE

I remember the first time I attempted to fix an old, broken axe. It was when I was living with friends at a farmhouse in the Slocan Valley, a small mountain town region of British Columbia. There were a lot of people in the area who used wood as a heat source, whether as a first source in an off-grid cabin in the mountainside or as a secondary source for a modern home closer to town.

In the valley, the snow cover would average 16 inches (40 cm) in the winter, with some days reaching 51 inches (130 cm) in December through February. The winter temperatures ranged from 41°F to –13°F (5°C to –25°C). At the farmhouse, it was always nice waking up to the living room woodstove warming up the home on a chilly winter morning. Whoever woke up first was the one to start the fire.

The woodstove was a central part of the home, and of course with a woodstove comes a woodpile and axes for chopping. Beside the farmhouse was a woodshed with a chopping block inside and axes hanging on the open walls. One of the splitting mauls had a loose head and a handle that seemed to have gotten into a few fights with knotted wood, which meant it wasn't getting used out of fear the axe head would fly off while swinging or the handle would snap upon too much impact.

Timeworn relics: rusted axe heads telling tales of hard labor, awaiting an eager hand to restore their former glory.

I googled how to rehandle an axe and decided to give it a go. It seemed simple enough. First, I cut off the handle by the shoulder of the axe. I grabbed a drywall saw and started sawing until the wood handle broke off. Next, I had to get the remaining wood out of the axe's eye. This took way longer than I assumed it would and brought more frustration than I anticipated. There was a metal wedge in the axe's eye that was keeping the remaining wood locked in. In my first attempt, I put the axe on the woodshed chopping block and grabbed a chisel and hammer to try pounding out the wood and metal wedge. That didn't work so well; the axe would fly here and there with each pound, and the clog of wood and metal wasn't budging. After my arm got tired from seemingly pointless chisel hammering, I went looking for a drill and vise. We had a vise in the garden shed, so I used that to secure the axe. Then, I found my roommate's drill and began to drill into the wood

around the metal wedge to loosen it up. I won't bore you with all the details of my mistakes during that attempt (doing so would take up the whole chapter!), but I will say it was frustrating and took me the whole day to figure out. Now, my process is smooth and efficient. I've also switched back to the good ol' hammer and chisel method. That's not to say I don't still make mistakes or have spontaneous ideas that don't work out, but through more time and appreciation for axe restoration, the process has become more and more enjoyable and expansive.

Our axe does a lot of work for us. It's one of the most resilient and reliable tools. Due to the labor it performs in outdoor conditions and the impact it takes, your axe can use a little TLC from time to time. Let's go through some tutorials on how to keep your axe in good shape so it is sharp and ready to swing. We'll take your axe through a three-part process of restore, revise (a.k.a. revitalize), and rest.

STAGE 1: RESTORE

Got an old wood axe with a broken handle? Or maybe you picked one up at a garage sale or antique shop? That axe has probably done a lot of hard work and still has a lot more hard work left in it. So let's keep that axe swinging by bringing some life back into that old tool. First, we'll need some tools to restore this tool. There are many different ways you can restore your axe, and lots of things you can use.

BARE-BONES MATERIALS

Chisel:	To get the old wood and metal out of the axe's eye
Hammer:	To use with the chisel and to mount the axe head on the new handle
Coarse and fine sandpaper:	To help shape the handle for fitting the axe head and to sand off rust from the axe head after de-rusting
Wood wedge:	You can make your own wood wedge with scrap wood or buy one at your local hardware store.
New handle:	There are a lot of premade hickory handles available at your local hardware store; make sure to get one that will fit your axe head and be a length you can "handle."
Finishing oil:	Boiled linseed oil is recommended for ample protection and to enhance the beauty of the grain.

NICE-TO-HAVE MATERIALS

Power drill:	To remove the remaining wood and metal from the axe's eye
Farrier rasp:	To shave off some wood to shape the handle
Electric belt sander or grinder:	To speed up the handle shaping and sharpening steps
Handsaw:	To cut off the remaining handle if there is still a bit of length
Vise or clamps:	To secure your axe head for old handle removal and sharpening
Metal wedge:	Putting in a metal wedge with the wood wedge will help add an extra lock to keep your axe head in place
Wood glue:	To put on the wood wedge to help secure it in the axe's eye
Draw knife:	To help sharpen the axe handle

Step 1: Remove the Old Handle and Clean Out the Axe Eye

Secure the axe in a vise or clamp it to a stable surface.

If there are more than a few inches of the handle left, start by sawing off the handle near the axe head to make it more manageable. Once the handle is sawed off, then comes the tricky part: cleaning out the axe's eye. Looking into the axe's eye can be very telling of the tool's work history. Usually you will see a wood wedge, but possibly also some metal wedges such as a nail, screw, or whatever the previous owner could jam in that hole to keep the head on. It's common to find a progression moving from a nice-looking wood wedge all the way down to some nails that were lying around and became wedges in a pinch. One thing's for sure, though: the more metal that's in the eye, the harder it will be to clean out the eye.

Now drill into the eye to loosen up the wood. If you want to do this old school or you don't have a drill, this is where you'll use the chisel and hammer to attack the wood in the eye. Decluttering the eye is usually the longest and most frustrating part of the process. I'll admit a few four-letter words have slipped out when the remaining wood wasn't surrendering. But once you're able to see right through the eye, you'll feel a special sort of satisfaction.

Clear out the old mess to make a fresh start for a timeless tool.

Rust on axes occurs due to a process called oxidation, which is a chemical reaction between iron, oxygen, and moisture.

SAFETY FIRST

I once used other axe heads to secure an axe by driving two axe heads into a wood round on either side of the axe I wanted to secure. There is always a way to get things done but always be careful. If you aren't able to do the job safely, wait until you have the tools and workstation you need to get the job done right.

Step 2: De-rust

If you're reading this section, it's likely that your axe isn't as shiny as it once was. Over the years of working outdoors, it's probably gathered some rust. Axe heads are usually made of medium- to high-carbon steel. The higher the carbon in the steel, the more corrosive it tends to be. There are many things you can use to remove the layer of rust, and some of these things you may already have in your cupboards.

1 HOUR IN VINEGAR

3 DAYS IN VINEGAR

Soak #1: Vinegar

To loosen up the rust on your axe head, try a vinegar soak. Place your axe head in a container large enough to submerge it. Pour white vinegar over the axe so that it's completely covered. Leave the axe head soaking for 24 hours or longer. Once the axe has soaked, you can use a wire brush, sandpaper, or steel wool to scrub off the rust. It will be messy, so you might also want to grab a clean cloth to wipe off the rust between sandings. Once you're satisfied with your cleaning, spray some WD-40 or a rust-protection spray on your axe head to keep it in good condition. You can also use regular olive oil for temporary protection if you don't have rust protection. Alternatively, you can mix some baking soda with water and give the axe a wash. This will neutralize the vinegar and prevent corrosion.

Soak #2: Coke Classic (the Kind with Real Sugar)

Similar to the vinegar soak, find a container that can submerge the axe head. Fill the container with some Coke Classic (Classic works better than Diet for some reason). Let the axe head sit fully submerged in the Coke for 24 hours. Once the Coke bath is done, use a wire brush, sandpaper, or steel wood to scrub off the rust. Now, we'll want to keep the rust off the axe. Either wipe down the axe with some baking soda and water, spray on some WD-40, or if you're in a pinch, use some olive oil. Be sure to cover the axe evenly with your protective product and wipe off any access liquid. (*Note:* Another fun use for Coke Classic is to remove the smell from animals who had an unfortunate run-in with a skunk.)

Soak #3: Citric Acid Powder

You can find citric acid powder in the canning and baking section of your local grocery store. First dissolve the powder in some warm water and make sure it's mixed thoroughly. Place your axe head in the solution so it's completely covered. Let it sit for 24 hours. If you've read the paragraphs for the previous two soaks, you'll know what comes next. After 24 hours in the citric acid, scrub off the rust with a wire brush, sandpaper, or steel wool. Finally, apply some rust protection (WD-40, baking soda and water, or olive oil) and wipe off any excess solution so the axe is completely dry.

No matter which soak solution you choose, soak the axe head for 24 hours to make the de-rusting easier.

Step 3: Fit the Handle

Premade handles from your hardware store probably won't fit exactly to the shape of your axe's eye. To get it shaped

STEEL RULER HACK

Remember those steel rulers you had in grade school? I bet you didn't think about their ability to shape wood. Because they are able to bend, they can emulate a drawknife. It won't be as sharp as a drawknife, but if you don't have many other uses for a drawknife and you happen to have a steel ruler in your drawer, give it a try.

Sometimes you'll get lucky and need to do only a bit of sanding to fit an axehead. Other times, you might need to strip away more wood. Keep in mind that there are different shapes to an axe's eye, such as a circle or a teardrop.

up, grab a marker and place the axe head on top of the handle. Trace the shape of the axe's eye onto the top of the handle. If you need to scrape off a few millimeters of wood to fit the shape, you can use a few tools.

Drawknife

This is a traditional woodworking tool made to shave off wood and bark. You use this tool by drawing the blade toward you—as the name suggests—and removing the wood shavings during the draw motion. Unless you are just finessing the fit, it's common to start here and work your way down to rasp and sandpaper.

Farrier Rasp

This tool works great for filing off the excess wood if there is only a small amount to remove. If you get lucky with fit, you may even be able to start with a rasp.

Coarse Sandpaper

When you get down to the point where there's just a minimal amount of wood to remove, sandpaper is best to get the perfect fit. I use very coarse sandpaper (around 60 grit).

Step 4: Hang the Axe

It's time to hang the axe! How do you know when you have the right fit? When the head is placed on the handle, you should be able to flip it upside down without the axe head falling off. If the axe head falls off when you flip it, the fitting might be too loose. If it's loose, no problem; just scooch the axe down the handle, closer to the shoulder, to make it a bit more snug. You might lose a bit of the shoulder area but at least you'll have a secure axe.

Once you're able to flip it without the head coming loose, take a soft-face hammer and hit the bottom of the handle, where the knob is. This force will drive the axe head up the handle to make it nice and tight to the wood. This is why rehandling an axe is sometimes called "hanging an axe" because you are hanging the axe on the handle.

Step 5: Wedge

The last thing you want to happen when you're chopping is for your axe head to go flying off your handle. Enter the final step in this process: wedging the head in place.

Wood Wedge: You can make your own wedge out of whatever wood you have lying around, though you do want something strong (and ideally a good-looking wood). Note that even if you use a metal wedge (which I'll get to in a minute), you'll drive a wood wedge in first. Take a small piece of wood that is the same length as the axe eye and taper it so that it becomes narrow with a wider top. As a person who lives in the Pacific Northwest, I've been fond of using arbutus wood for my wedges. Not only is it beautiful and strong, but it also adds a bit of my home island as a signature to the axes I work.

The wedge is driven into a slot that has been cut into the top of the handle during the manufacturing process. Sometimes, the wedge doesn't fit fully in the slot, which means you may need to take your handsaw and cut off the excess wood sticking out of the top. While you're driving the wood wedge in, be cautious not to use too much force or you'll break the wood as it's fitting into the kerf. If you do break it, no worries. You can add more wood into the crack of the broken wedge, which might create a bit of a cool design.

Metal Wedge: If you want an extra bit of security, you can buy a metal wedge to add after the wood wedge. A metal wedge is optional but also recommended so your axe head is super secure on the handle. Metal wedges typically come in the shape of either a triangle or a circle. To set a metal wedge, find the center of the axe's eye. For the triangle metal wedge, you'll want to go across the wood wedge so it locks the wood wedge into the handle. For a circle metal wedge, drive it into the center of the axe eye so it's circling over part of the wood wedge and wood from the handle.

Step 6: Finish and Protect

Before we seal and protect the axe, let's slip in another step of revision. Here is where you can choose your own adventure and jump to the staining section of this chapter to explore some options for adorning your axe in the form of adding color, or you can continue on to the finishing and protecting steps. Once you have your axe fitted and secured (and stained, if preferred), it's time to finish it off with a bit of beauty and protection.

Boiled Linseed Oil: To protect the handle, I like to use boiled linseed oil. Not only does the oil add a protective coating to the wood, but it also enhances the natural beauty of the grain. Linseed oil is extracted from flaxseed. When applying linseed oil to your axe handle, make sure to use gloves. Apply one to three coats to the handle with a rag. Wipe off any access oil and let it dry. (WARNING: Linseed oil will generate heat as it dries and has the potential to combust if left on a wet rag. Before using the oil, make sure you read the bottle for methods of proper rag disposal after use. Ideally, hand wash the rags before storing them in a metal container until they can be properly disposed of.)

Alternatively, if you don't want to use a combustable oil, there are other options.

Beeswax: Slather some warm beeswax onto your handle and rub it into the wood until you have a nice even coat. Buff it with a clean cloth and let it dry for a full day before using your axe. You'll need to apply wax more frequently than linseed oil. Apply a layer of wax when you start to feel the wood grain of the handle.

Cutting Board Oil: This oil is food-safe and won't self-combust. Rub some oil into the handle until it's completely covered. This oil might need a few coats to get it to a good protection level for your handle. It may also need to be reapplied monthly or whenever you can feel the grain of your axe.

STAGE 2: REVISE
(A.K.A. REVITALIZE)

Now that your axe is handled and restored, let's add some revisions to your tool. This is where you can add elements of creativity and/or practicality. Adorning and adding a personal touch to tools has long been a historic and cultural practice (see chapter 1).

Now, you might not be taking your axe on a journey through enchanted landscapes and battling mythical creatures (or maybe you are? I don't assume to know your hobbies . . .). Either way, this tool will be your noble sidekick through your quest of slaying knotted pine, breaking dense grain, and relentlessly chopping a dwindling pile of kindling. Ultimately, your axe is the key on your mission of bringing warmth and light to you and your comrades, so why not honor it with a personal touch?

Step 1

Step 2

Overstrike Wrap

Wrapping an axe handle can help improve grip and control while also protecting the handle from wear and tear. Paracord, nylon cord, and leather lace are great materials to use for wrapping. I've even used a few layers of hockey tape; it's the easiest material to apply and does a decent job protecting the handle.

To wrap the handle, get some 3 mm paracord. Wrap it around the shoulder and top of the axe's belly to protect it from overstrikes (where you miss your target and the wood of the axe makes contact with the target instead of the axe's blade; this is where a lot of injuries to the axe occur).

Step 1: To begin, wrap your overstrike protection area with hockey tape or cloth tape to help the paracord stay in place while you wrap. Take your paracord and fold it onto the axe so it's the desired length of your overstrike protection. Make sure to have one shorter end of the fold by the axe head and one longer end of the uncut paracord.

Step 2: Begin wrapping the longer end of the paracord around the shorter end starting from the top by the axe head. Keep part of the shorter paracord exposed at the top so it's the length of the axe head. Try to make your first wrap layer nice and tight to the axe metal.

Step 3: Continue wrapping down around the handle and over the folded paracord strips. We will tighten it up in the end, so keep your wraps tight but not too tight.

Step 3

Step 4: Once your wrap comes close to the end of the folded paracord, leave that fold exposed. Take the long wrapping paracord strip and cut it to half the length of the overstrike protection length.

Step 5: Take your cut paracord end and draw it through the exposed fold.

Step 4

Step 5

Step 6

Step 6: Here's where it all comes together. Take that top paracord end and pull. The pull will bring the bottom paracord under the wrap and tighten everything. The bottom paracord may need to be fed through some of the wrap layers because it might get stuck. Pull until the bottom paracord is at least one-third of the way up the wrap or until it's tight enough not to move.

Step 7: Once your wrap is tight, you can knot the ends if you have enough material, then cut off the excess paracord and secure the ends with a dab of sealing glue. You can also use a lighter to melt and seal the ends of the paracord so it doesn't fray and then tuck the ends into the wrap.

Step 7

MYTHICAL BLADES
AND
WEAPONS

Warriors would frequently name their weapons to create a bond between the weapon and its owner. It was a sign of honor and respect for an item carried into battle. The naming of weapons and tools has also inspired legends and stories. Let's take a look at a few legendary blades for inspiration.

Excalibur: Excalibur is the legendary sword of King Arthur. There are two predominant stories about the origin of Excalibur. In one version, it is the sword pulled from the stone by Arthur that gives him claims to the throne of Britain. In another legend, the sword is given to Arthur by the Lady of the Lake. In all origin stories, Excalibur is said to have extraordinary power, making Arthur invincible in battle. Excalibur is often seen as a symbol of leadership and bravery.

Artemis's Bow and Arrow: Artemis is the Greek goddess of hunting. She has an impressive catalog of weapons, including a quiver, hunting spears, and most famously, her enchanted bow and arrows. In some myths, her arrows were said to cause sudden and painless death, reflecting her role as a death-dealer and a protector who could swiftly end suffering. Artemis's bow and arrows were more than just weapons; they were symbols of her divine power.

Hrunting: This sword was known for its strength and reliability in battle as depicted in the Anglo-Saxon poem *Beowulf*. Unfortunately, the sword fails Beowulf in the battle against Grendel's mother (spoiler alert), but Beowulf finds another weapon to defeat the antagonist, showing the importance of human adaptability and determination to finish the mission rather than relying too much on a fancy weapon to do the job.

Stormbreaker: This axe-hammer is from the Thor Marvel comics and was inspired by Norse mythology. The Stormbreaker is made of mystic Uru metal and is said to be indestructible. It is a symbol of pure strength.

Sting: From the world of J. R. R. Tolkien, Sting was a shortened sword crafted by elves. The character Bilbo Baggins took Sting on his epic journey to the dwarven kingdom of Erebor to help the dwarves reclaim their home from the dragon Smaug. Later in the saga, Sting is passed on to Frodo Baggins to assist him on his quest to Mount Doom.

These iconic blades represent themes that continue to be passed down in modern tales of bravery, leadership, and connecting with your inner strength. The blades are respected and honored through their quest with the people and beings who wield them.

Staining

Want to add a bit of creative splash to your axe handle? There's no need for previous training in the art of staining wood for furniture. Axe handles are a much smaller job, and you can experiment with a variety of materials to give them some additional character.

Staining needs to happen before you apply any protective oil to the handle. Some store-bought handles might already have a protective coat or finish applied; if so, sand off that layer of protection before staining your handle. If your handle is completely raw, you'll still need to condition it for staining by opening the pores of the wood. Start with some fine-grit sandpaper such as 180 or higher and give a light sanding all over the handle. Liberally rub down the handle with some warm water. The warm water will raise the grain and make it easier for the wood to take in the stain. Make sure your handle is clean and dampened with the water before applying the stain. You'll only need to raise the grain with water and sanding for water-based stains like the ones on the coming pages.

COFFEE AND WINE

You've probably placed your coffee cup on a wooden table only to find a classic circular coffee stain later, which means you're familiar with the staining capabilities of coffee on wood. So, these first stains will make a lot of sense. Perhaps you've also been with friends and a bottle of red wine only to end up laughing so hard at your friend's story about her mom's three-legged cat that some of the wine spilled out of the glass and onto your other friend's white pants (I swear that wasn't my own experience). So, as we have all encountered, there are a lot of beverages and things in our homes that can leave a good, deep stain.

Instant Coffee: Take 2 to 3 tablespoons (16 to 24 g) of instant coffee and add 3 tablespoons (45 ml) of boiling water. Stir it up until it's a thick paint-like texture. Use a sponge or cloth to apply the coffee all over the handle. Let the coffee sit on the handle for 20 to 30 minutes and then wipe off the coffee and let the handle dry. You can repeat this process until the handle takes on your desired coffee tone.

Espresso Shot: Brew up a strong espresso, take a sniff—because coffee smells amazing and makes you happy—and then apply it right to your handle using a sponge, soft paintbrush, or cloth. This will take a lot of repeat applications due to the amount of water in the espresso shot. The stronger the shot, the easier the staining.

Tea: Not a coffee drinker? No problem. Just like coffee, brewed tea can also be used as a stain. Black tea will work best because it is high in tannins, which will create a reaction with the tannins in the wood for a more pronounced stain. To create a black tea stain, brew three tea bags in 2 cups (480 ml) of boiled water. Allow the mixture to sit for four times the duration it says on the box. Or do my classic method, set it and forget it—until you reenter your kitchen and remember you're making a stain. Once the tea has been so over-brewed it becomes offensive to an Englishman, take a sponge, soft paintbrush, or cloth and slather it onto your handle. You'll probably have to repeat the staining application a few times to get the right tea color tone. You can also try it with different types of teas. Some teas that have fewer tannins, such as oolong and green tea, will take a

few more applications until you start to see the staining on the wood.

Red Wine: Are you a fan of mulled wine? Maybe invite your axe over for an evening of wine; it could be physically transformative for it. To make wine stain, pour a bottle of wine into a saucepan. Bring it to almost a boil and then let it simmer for 2 to 3 hours. Once it's been simmering and a portion of the water has evaporated, it should be concentrated enough to be ready to apply to the axe handle. Grab a sponge, soft paintbrush, or cloth and liberally slather the handle with the warmed wine. Let it dry after your first coat and repeat if necessary. This can be a dramatic treatment because it will give the handle a bright red color. If you have some wine still simmering in your saucepan after staining, add some brandy, orange slices, cinnamon, and clove and enjoy a traditional beverage as you admire your work. Cheers to you!

Coffee: nectar of the gods, spark of life, and a great wood stain

Onion Skins: Compost or creative stain option? You decide. After dinner, take your onion skins and boil them. You'll want to have at least a handful of onion skins to make enough stain for an axe handle. The skins will create a stain with a shade of orange, brown, or reddish-brown. The color tone may vary depending on the type and age of the onions you're using. Put the onion skins in a saucepan and cover them with water so they are completely submerged. Bring the water to a light boil, cover the pot, and let it simmer for at least an hour or until the water starts to color. You can also let the skins sit overnight after simmering to allow them to release more color. Once you have your concentration prepared, apply the mix to the handle with a sponge, soft paintbrush, or cloth.

Vinegar and Steel Wool: Grab a mason jar and put two steel wool pads inside. Pour 2 to 3 cups (480 to 720 ml) of white vinegar in the mason jar so that the pads are completely submerged. Close the jar and allow that mixture to sit for 24 hours to a few days (or forget about it like I usually do and allow it to sit for a few weeks until you remember it again). The mixture will then be nice and potent for wood staining. When you're ready to stain, put on some rubber or vinyl gloves because this mixture will stain your hands. Also be warned, it will have a very pungent smell, so open the jar slowly and maybe hold your breath. Take one of the steel wool pads—which is probably very mushy after soaking in acid for so long—and apply the mixture to your axe handle. Make sure the coat is even and your axe handle has been completely covered with your stain. This vinegar-steel combo will have an amber, caramel tone when it's first applied to the handle, and as it dries, it turns a grayish-purple. The handle will turn this interesting color combination because it's likely made of hickory, which is a low-tannin wood. Tannins are an acidic chemical found in sap and will influence the reaction to some stains. Woods that are high in tannins, like walnut and oak, will turn a darker tone with this vinegar-steel combo.

Mix It Up!

Once you've gotten into staining with all these ingredients on their own, you can also have some fun with staining combinations. I once stained an axe with instant coffee but then wanted a more pronounced grain and a dynamic color tone, so I did a layer of vinegar and steel. The result was an amplified grain texture with a warmer grayish-purple tone. I've also brewed up some red wine and berry herbal tea into a concentrated mixture that gave a darker purple tone to the stain. Staining is one of my favorite parts of the process because you can use whatever you have in your pantry to experiment with, and if you don't like the results, simply sand off the layer of stain from your handle and try again.

When staining with beets, things might get messy.

Sharpen

If the blade on your axe has dulled, it can feel as though you're chopping with a hammer. Axes are designed for cutting, so maintaining the proper blade is crucial. Interestingly, a blade doesn't need to be razor-sharp to chop wood effectively. In fact, if the blade is too sharp, it can bury itself too deep into the wood, making it more likely to get stuck. When it comes to sharpening, you can choose between a file, a sharpening stone, or a belt sander. A belt sander is faster but requires more skill to avoid overheating the blade or sanding off too much material, while a file or sharpening stone allows for more tactile control and intention with every stroke. It's always wise to master sharpening by hand before moving on to power tools like the belt sander.

File: A dual-sided file around 9 inches (23 cm) will do the trick. One side of the file will have double-cut teeth and feel rougher. This side will help if you want to remove any noticeable nicks from the blade or to do some reshaping. The other side of the file will be single-cut teeth that can be used for finer sharpening.

Begin by stabilizing the axe with a vice or by clamping the axe to a table. If your axe is in need of a full sharpening procedure, start with the double-cut side of the file. Hold the file at a consistent angle (usually 25 to 30 degrees) against the edge of the axe blade. Push the file across the edge, starting from the axe's heel to the toe in smooth, even strokes.

Keep even pressure for the strokes, maintaining consistent contact to make sure you're removing any nicks or dull spots. Count the number of strokes so you can repeat them on the other side. Once you're happy with the feel of the blade from using the double-cut side for the file, flip it to the single-cut side to refine and finish.

Sharpening Stone: Similar to a file, one side of a sharpening stone is rougher for more acute sharpening and material removal, and the other side is for more precision sharpening and refining. Let's start with the rougher side. Apply a few drops of honing oil or water to the surface of the sharpening stone to reduce unwanted friction. Hold the stone at a consistent angle against the axe (usually 25 to 30 degrees). Starting from the heel of the axe, move in small, circular motions along the edge. Work along the entire length of the blade. Count your reps to repeat on the other side. Start with 3 reps on each side until you feel happy with the evenness and edge angle. Flip the stone over to the finer side and repeat the circular motion along the edge. Start with 3 reps on each side of the axe with the finer side of the stone. Repeat until you are satisfied with your blade.

Sharpening with a file.

Belt Sander: If you are feeling confident with the sharpening techniques of using a file and stone and are ready to explore some power sharpening, let's talk about belt sanders.

A belt sander is a pivotal tool for anyone who makes and restores blades. It's a powerful tool that can get the job done in no time but can also do some harm to the blade if it's not used properly. For instance, if you hold the blade on the sander for too long, it can overheat the metal and change the temper of the blade. This will make the metal softer and cause it to lose some toughness. When using a belt sander, have a bucket of water close by so you can continuously dunk the axe head in the water to keep it from overheating. You also want to use safety goggles because there could be some rogue metal pieces flying off your axe as you sand.

To start, use a black marker and mark the area on your blade you want to sharpen. This will help you know where the sander is making contact with metal when you're guiding the blade on the belt. Turn on the sander and carefully guide the axe blade against the belt and on a slight angle. Move the blade back and forth from heel to toe to evenly sharpen the edge. Avoid overheating the blade by being consistent with your sanding stroke and dipping it in water frequently or taking breaks to let it cool down. Keep checking the edge for sharpness and evenness so you're not taking off too much material. Once you are happy with the initial sharpening, you can get more refined by changing the belt to a finer grit level (120 to 150) to hone the edge further.

At left: Sharpening with a sharpening stone. Above: Sharpening with a belt sander.

Razor Sharp

After sharpening, carefully feel the edge of the axe with your fingertip to check for any burrs or rough or uneven spots. Burrs are a very small and thin strip of metal that folds over the edge and makes the blade uneven at its peak. To remove burrs, use the finer side of the file or sharpening stone until the edge is even.

Leather Strop

If necessary, use a leather strop to remove any burrs and refine the edge further. A leather strop is made from thick, high-quality leather and usually comes mounted to a wooden base for a stable flat surface. The leather strop is used to refine and polish an edge and remove any remaining burrs from a blade.

To use the strop, place the edge of the blade on the strop facing away from you and at a 20-degree angle. Gently draw the blade backward and at a diagonal. Keep light pressure as you glide the blade; too much pressure can cause the edge to roll or the leather to wear unevenly. Flip the blade and repeat the process on the other side.

STAGE 3: REST

After a hard day's work of chopping and firewood prep, you and your axe might need some rest and recovery. To keep your axe in good shape, make sure its resting place is sheltered from the rain and has airflow to prevent moisture buildup. Too much moisture will lead to rust on your axe head and your wood handle won't be too pleased either. Axe heads are typically made of medium- to high-carbon steel, which has a higher chance of rusting than your stainless steel cooking pot.

When you're done using your axe for the day, wipe it down and spray on some WD-40 to add a layer of rust protection. Ideally, your axe will live in your woodshed, keeping it off the ground and sheltered. This way, your axe is near the materials you'll be using it for and it'll be ready to go when it's chopping time.

WHAT IS AN AXE MADE OF?

Axes are made from various types of steel, which is a combination of carbon and iron. Specific alloys of steel have additional ingredients added to them to improve strength, hardness, toughness, or corrosion resistance. Medium- or high-carbon alloy steels are common choices for axe heads. These alloys are also called tool steels. They are designed to withstand high impact and wear, making them suitable for heavy-duty axes used in forestry, construction, and outdoor activities.

To get more specific, when steel has a higher percentage of carbon (between 0.60 and 1.5 percent), its hardness, strength, and wear resistance is increased. It's common to use medium- and high-carbon alloy steels for knives, axes, springs, and automotive components. The more carbon present in the steel, the more it will require more particular methods for working with that tool. High-carbon steel is also more susceptible to corrosion and rust when compared to low-carbon steel, especially in environments with high humidity or exposure to moisture. This is why your axe is very susceptible to getting that layer of rust if left out in the rain. If you have an axe that easily gets rusty, simply applying some oil, WD-40, or rust protection spray to the axe head will help keep the steel in good shape and keep it shiny longer.

On the other hand, low-carbon steel (up to 0.30 percent) is less corrosive and tends to be easier to weld and work with. Low-carbon steel is used for construction pipes, machinery, and food cans. It is also more cost-effective to use low-carbon steel due to the higher maintenance manufacturing of high-carbon steel.

To get even deeper into the elements, an alloy steel called 5160 is a common choice for chopping blades and automotive parts. It has a carbon presence of 0.64 percent. It offers toughness but isn't very corrosion resistant.

5160 STEEL BREAKDOWN:

MANGANESE:

1.00%

Amplifies
hardness

CHROMIUM:

0.90%

Increases corrosion
resistance

CARBON:

0.64%

Helps the blade retain its edge
and increases hardness

SILICON:

0.30%

Increases
heat resistance

PHOSPHORUS:

0.04%

Improves tooling ability and
increases hardness

SULFUR:

0.04%

Makes tooling
easier

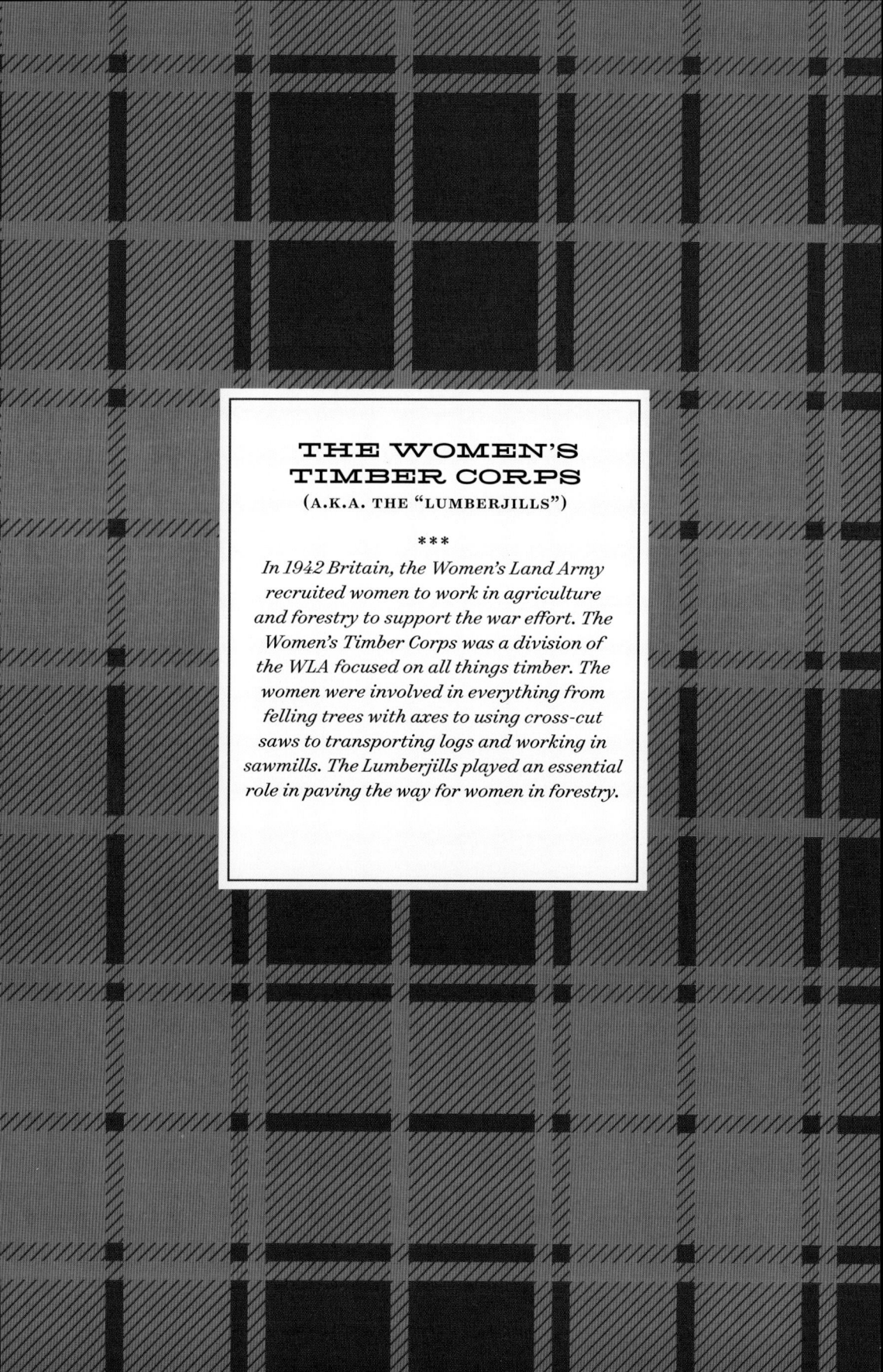

THE WOMEN'S TIMBER CORPS

(A.K.A. THE "LUMBERJILLS")

***

In 1942 Britain, the Women's Land Army recruited women to work in agriculture and forestry to support the war effort. The Women's Timber Corps was a division of the WLA focused on all things timber. The women were involved in everything from felling trees with axes to using cross-cut saws to transporting logs and working in sawmills. The Lumberjills played an essential role in paving the way for women in forestry.

CHAPTER 4

INTO THE WOODS

It's inevitable that the more you chop wood, the more you'll get to know and understand the trees you're chopping. An unexpected benefit is that it has made my walks in the woods more vivid and stimulating. Being able to distinguish the different grains, leaves, and characteristics needed to identify tree species adds a new layer to any walk. Noticing when a tree has a disease and the signs of illness can be important. Even taking note of how many animals, fungi, and insects have homes in and on each tree and how interconnected the forest really is . . . there's nothing like it.

When it comes to using wood as a resource, the more you know about the wood and forest ecosystems in your area, the more respect you will have for taking that life from the forest and the more you will appreciate the gift it's bringing you.

While you may be tempted to skip this chapter and dive directly into chapter 5 to get right into firewood, I encourage you to continue reading this one for a more well-rounded view of this wonderful hobby.

IN THIS CHAPTER

Natural spaces awaken the senses, from the small detail of a bug crawling across a leaf to the vast landscapes of a never-ending mountain range. Listen to the choir of birds or the orchestra of wind and river. Touch the soft moss and rough bark or walk barefoot on a damp forest floor. Taste the salty sea air by the shoreline or forage some forest foods like wild fiddleheads. You don't even have to be in the woods to enjoy these sensations. Think of it the next time you smell the fresh earth after a rainstorm. You can feel more immersed in the natural world by simply noticing what is around through your senses.

That said, I think in nature most people *feel* more and become more present. Through that presence, you can take in more information from the forest to learn and observe. Maybe you want to start becoming a bit more intentional about your time and awareness in nature. Start with a focus. Focus on one of your senses. If this sounds abstract, here's an example: smell. When you're in a forest, what do you smell? Maybe it's many smells? Do you know what is causing the smell(s)? Does the smell change when you walk around? How many micro and macro smells are happening? What are the sources?

Focusing on one of your senses can take you on a whole journey through the forest and can open you up to new observations and stimulations you would usually never notice. All it takes is some intentional focus and a few reflective thoughts to start.

PETRICHOR

Do you notice when you're in a forest after a rainstorm that there is a pleasantly fresh, earthy smell? This smell is known as petrichor, and it's primarily a mixture of three things. One part is plant oils. During dry periods, plants secrete oils into the soil. When it rains, these oils are released into the air, contributing to the scent. Another contributor to the smell is geosmin. In the forest, geosmin is a compound produced by soil-dwelling bacteria and cyanobacteria. When it rains, the soil releases geosmin into the air, creating an earthy odor. Ozone may also be a contributor of petrichor. Ozone isn't always present in petrichor, but if there was a thunderstorm with the rain, the addition of UV light and electrical activity will produce ozone, which adds a sharpness to the scent. Humans may be evolutionarily predisposed to enjoy the smell of petrichor. The scent could signal the arrival of rain, which was crucial for survival, especially in arid regions.

Feel the Forest

I grew up in London, Ontario; it's a city called "the forest city." There's a bit of irony to that given name. The downtown core was decorated with around fifty multicolored metal trees that cost the city hundreds of thousands of dollars. Now I'm not opposed to paying for public art, but there was a lot of controversy that arose from the city spending so much on these tree sculptures as a way of honoring their forest city name, instead of putting the funds and intentions toward preserving the real forests that were shrinking with rapid development. Thankfully, I always had access to a forest. The home I grew up in was down the road from a wetland area. I was a shy kid and was okay with spending time on my own, especially in natural spaces. In nature, I never really felt alone. These spaces were my safe place, a place to dream, to explore, to process, to observe, to feel, to just be.

Since I developed that connection to nature as a kid, my relationship with it grew through the many stages of life. I found I would always gravitate toward spending some time in nature whenever I was going through something stressful in life. It became a soft place for me to fall when I felt I didn't have anywhere else to go to think and process. No one feels judged in a forest, no one feels that they must hide any thoughts or suppress emotions. You feel free to feel.

Back to those metal trees. Though art can provide spaces for reflection, observation, and many similarities to nature, in my opinion there is no comparison to the full immersion of being in a natural space and what that experience can offer you (if you let it). Here's a reflection question: The last time you were in a forest or any natural environment, what were you feeling? Were you aware of what was happening within you or was your focus on the external and what was happening around you? Did a certain sound, smell, or sight capture your attention? Nature is a place to stimulate awareness on any level.

FOREST TO FOREST:
MY OWN JOURNEY

Growing up in Ontario, I became familiar with ecosystems around the Great Lakes–St. Lawrence forest region and the boreal forest region. Maples and white birch were common around the area I lived in. There are a lot of deciduous trees in Ontario. Since deciduous trees seasonally shed their leaves, autumn is also an incredible display of vibrant colors. Raking leaves was also part of the to-do list at my family's home during the autumn months. The neighbor kids would make massive piles of leaves on the front lawns, and we'd all find the best one to jump in, sometimes bringing leaves from other lawns over to our chosen leaf

pile to grow it (something the adults weren't too fond of). Once winter rolls around and the snow begins to fall, there are barely any leaves left on the tree branches. Without leaves, the trees don't hold much of the snow that falls onto them, so the winter forests still have light coming in through the open canopies of the trees.

I moved to the interior of British Columbia in the summer of 2020, to the Kootenay region. One of the first things I noticed while exploring my new surroundings was how tall the trees were and how abundant evergreens (conifers) such as pine, spruce, and cedar are in the region. Most conifers don't seasonally spark color and

shed their needle-like leaves, but of course, there is an exception. Larch trees look like most conifers and have needle leaves, but they don't hold onto them all year. The needle-like leaves on a larch tree will turn a bright golden-yellow hue in the fall, and the leaves will shed for the winter, making this conifer-looking tree deciduous. Larch trees can be found growing up high on the mountainsides. When autumn rolls around, you'll see drops of golden hues speckled throughout the high mountain landscapes. It's a beautiful slight, especially if you hike up to the alpine to catch a closer glimpse of these flaming trees.

In 2023, I moved to a small island in the Pacific Northwest. Here, the oceanic climate allows for different trees to grow that wouldn't make it in the dry, rocky mountain climates of the interior or the humid temperatures of the Great Lakes–St. Lawrence region. When I began to explore my new coastal settling, a certain tree kept catching my eye. I noticed a tree growing around the shoreline slopes with twisty trunks and an orange-red color. If you've spent time by the coast, the arbutus trees are hard to miss. They are conifer trees, yet they have broad leaves like most deciduous trees. They do also shed, just not their leaves. Arbutus trees shed their bark: outer layers of their bark grow dry and then turn a darker brown color. It then peels off to reveal a new greenish layer underneath.

Throughout the regions I've lived in and spent a lot of time in, I always enjoy getting to know the local forests. It's always fascinating to notice the different characteristics of the trees and ecosystems within their unique environments.

IDENTIFYING TREES

Being able to identify trees can be a rewarding skill that enhances your connection to the forest. There are many aspects of trees you can observe to narrow down their species.

To identify trees, ask questions that help describe its aspects and characteristics. For instance, look at the shape of the leaf: Is it broad, flat, needle-like? Or perhaps even scale-like? Is the edge of the leaf flat or wavy? Take a look at how the leaves are arranged: Are they

TREE	LEAVES/NEEDLES	BARK	SEEDS
Oak	Lobed, often with a leathery texture	Rough and ridged, dark brown to gray	Acorns: Small and rounded with little hats, often found around the base of the tree
Maple	Distinct five lobes	Smooth when young, becoming rough with age	Seeds: Winged; they look like helicopters and are fun to make fly
Pine	Bundles of long, thin needles	Scaly and rough	Cones: Woody cones, varying in size
Cedar	Thin and scale-like	Soft and fibrous, easy to peel off the tree	Small and egg-shaped with scales in irregular clusters
Alder	Rounded with a serrated edge	Smooth when young, becoming slightly scaly with age	Male catkins are long, soft, and thin, hanging loosely in clusters from the branches. Female catkins are much smaller, more compact, and upright or slightly oval in shape, resembling tiny green pine cones.
Willow	Long, narrow, and lance-shaped	Smooth and gray when young, becoming furrowed with age	Catkins: Soft, furry flower clusters
Fir	Clusters of small needle-like leaves attached to the branch	Smooth and gray when young, becoming very thick and ridged as the tree grows	Cones: Softer than pine cones with scales that don't overlap

symmetrical or alternating? Is the leaf a single blade or are there multiple leaflets? And those are just questions about the leaves. There are many other parts of the tree we observe to find its identity, such as the bark, flowers, fruits, seeds, height and spread, and habitat, to name a few.

TYPE	HABITAT	FIREWOOD
Hardwood	Found across a wide range of regions	Slow-burning, with consistent heat and low smoke
Hardwood	Different varieties have adapted to a wide range of temperatures and environments but are mostly found in moist soils	Burns hot and clean, with low smoke
Softwood	Many pines are tolerant of extreme cold and higher elevations	Burns quickly with a lot of heat, and produces resinous sap that can cause creosote buildup in chimneys
Softwood	Likes wet soil in low to medium elevations	Burns fast and hot, ideal for kindling
Hardwood	Likes damp areas along streams and valleys	Very easy to chop compared to most other hardwoods, burns faster than other hardwoods but provides a reliable heat
Hardwood	Commonly found by rivers	Similar to a softwood, burning very hot and quickly
Softwood	From dry mountains to the temperate coast	One of the best softwoods to use as fuelwood, easy to light and burns longer than most softwoods

ANATOMY OF A LOG

When you come across a freshly cut stump, you'll notice a few different parts of the tree's interior. Knowing these parts of the tree can be useful for woodworking and especially for use as firewood. For example, if you're able to identify the heartwood of a tree, you'll know that it is the densest part of the tree and will burn longer than the wood closer to the bark.

Log Parts

A. Outer Bark: The shield of the tree that protects it from weather, disease, and insects.

B. Inner Bark (Phloem): Transports nutrients and sugars to other parts of the tree through photosynthesis.

C. Cambium: A thin layer of tissue between the bark and the wood. Fun fact: This is one of the most edible parts of the tree. If you're in a forest and need a fibrous snack, remove the layers of bark until you feel the thin and slimy cambium, then cut small sections and get ready for a lot of chewing.

D. Sapwood (Xylem): The younger wood that transports water and nutrients throughout the tree.

E. Heartwood: The inner wood that is denser than sapwood and darker in color. It no longer helps transport water and nutrients but plays a big part in providing structural support for the tree.

F. Pith: The very center and original growth of the tree. Sometimes it's spongy or softer.

Growth Rings

You'll also notice the iconic growth rings of the tree. Can you count them? A new ring will appear with each full growth cycle of the tree, which is approximately one year. Each growth ring will have two different color tones that represent the earlywood and latewood growth. Earlywood is lighter in color and wider; this is formed during the spring, when growth is more rapid. Latewood is darker and narrower. This is when growth is slowing down during the summer and fall.

Dendrochronology is the study of tree rings. Examining a crosscut section of a tree can give us a lot of information about the tree and the forest. For example, if some rings are abnormally narrow, this could suggest a period of drought and nutrient deficiency. The presence of disease and insects can create some irregular patterns in the rings as well. The growth rings provide a record of the past, and through studying the information from the rings, we can track changes in climate and monitor the health of a forest.

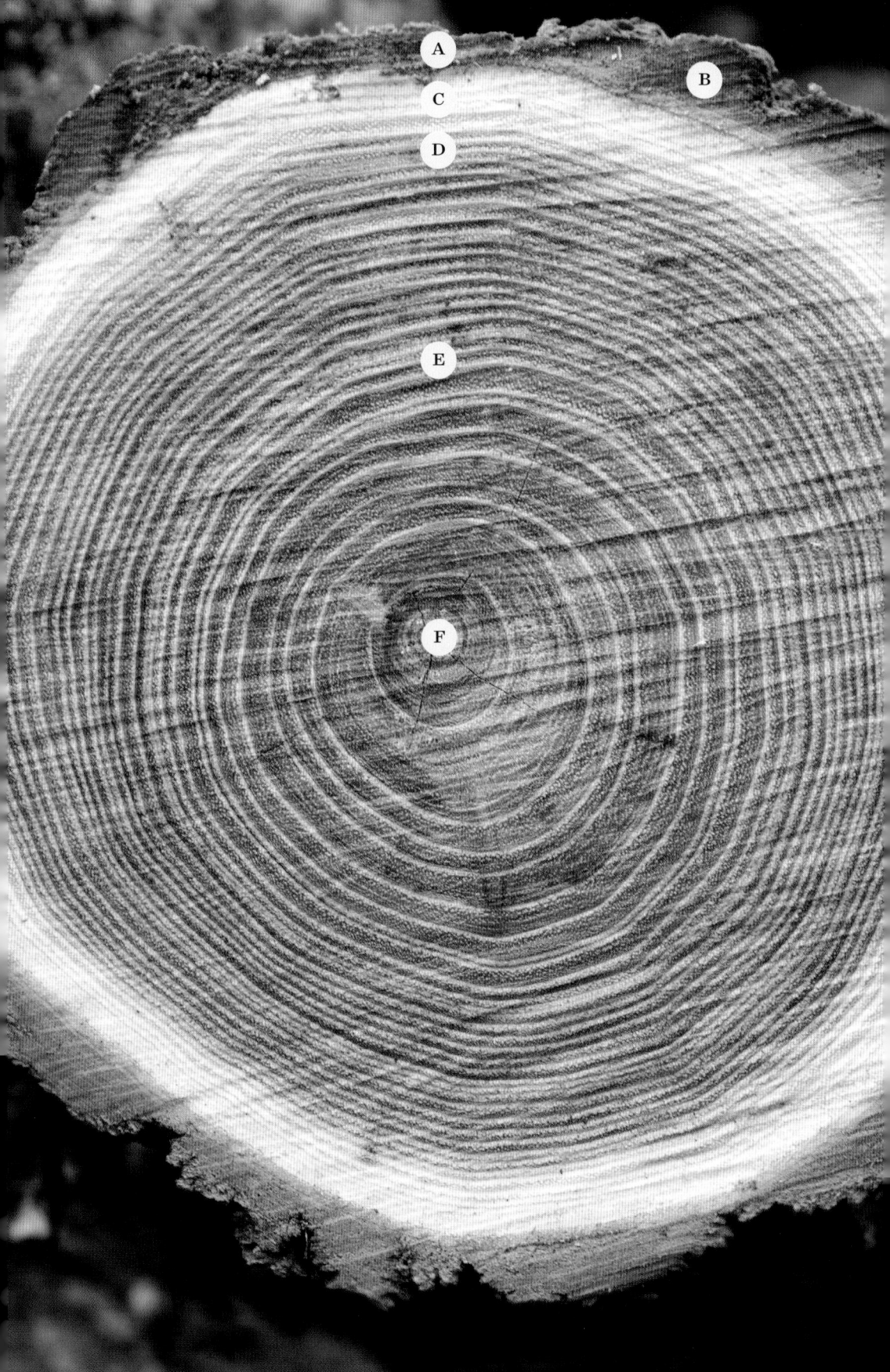

HARVESTING A TREE

There are many considerations that go into harvesting a tree for firewood. Some methods should be taken on only by a trained professional. It's also always best practice to never go harvesting alone. You're working with axes and chainsaws, which can cause some serious damage to the human body if something goes wrong. Always have a buddy with you! (It also makes the experience more fun.)

Where to Harvest Your Own Trees for Firewood

Harvesting your own firewood in North America involves many considerations. First, make sure you're complying with local regulations, using sustainable practices, and being aware of personal safety. Here's a guide to help you through the process.

Permits Required: In many states, provinces, and territories, you need a permit to harvest firewood from public land. These permits are often available through government offices. There are usually restrictions on the amount of wood you can harvest and specific areas where you can or cannot cut down trees.

Sustainable Practices: Regulations often emphasize sustainable harvesting practices to ensure environmental protection.

Private Land: Even if you own your own land, you must comply with local bylaws and regulations, which may have restrictions around felling trees on your property.

Protected Areas: Cutting down trees in national parks, provincial parks, and other protected areas is typically prohibited to preserve natural ecosystems.

What happens when small groups of people take trees illegally? Well, to see how that can escalate, let me tell you about the timber mafia. Yes, there are rings of criminal groups targeting and trafficking high-value trees to sell illegally. You've probably heard about wildlife poaching, people killing animals such as rhinos for their high-value horns. Their aim is solely profit driven and their tactics are usually cruel and without a second thought about the animal and the ecosystem's welfare. When poaching escalates and there aren't strong systems in place to prevent it, we end up losing members of our ecosystems. Over 90 percent of the black rhino population was wiped out from 1970 to 1990 due to poaching.

Before the fur trade in North America, the beaver population was estimated to be over 150 million. When the fur trade began to expand and evolve in the 1600s and continue for over 200 years, it didn't have the beavers' best interest in mind. Due to high demand for beaver fur and the products it produced, such as beaver fur hats, the beaver population was almost completely wiped out in North America. Ironically, the beaver is a significant symbol of Canada and has become a mascot for the country that massacred so many of them. Thankfully, there are initiatives in place to protect beavers and help them build back their population. Of course, climate change and various other factors are making beaver revitalization a bit more challenging, but the beavers—being the resilient and determined creatures they are—are bouncing back!

If we completely lost these furry little wetland engineers, it would have a devastating impact on other animals and water systems. Beavers build dams across streams and rivers, creating ponds and wetlands. These wetlands provide habitats for a wide range of plant and animal species, including fish, amphibians, birds, and insects. The beavers build infrastructure that also helps create a water-filtration system. The dams help trap pollutants and sediments, preventing them from being washed downstream. They also remove excess nutrients like nitrogen and phosphorus from the water, which helps reduce the risk of harmful algal blooms. I could go on about how impressive and hardworking beavers are. I'll end my Beaver TED Talk by encouraging you to go to a wetland area and see the beavers' work in action.

Similarly, tree poaching is a crime that has devastating impacts on the immediate ecosystem and beyond. Tree poaching refers to the illegal harvesting or removal of trees from forests, parks, or private properties. As consumers of wood furniture, wood décor, and other wood products, we rarely think about where that material comes from. With supply chains being so global and having so many hands in production, it's hard to track the sources of these materials and verify the suitability of the product. This means there is a lot of opportunity for industries to cut corners in favor of cutting manufacturing time and costs instead of implementing more sustainable practices. But poaching usually starts smaller than big industries.

Tree poaching has become an issue in communities that previously relied on the logging industry for jobs. Once those jobs are gone it can cause a lot of financial stress on the people of that community. When people are desperate, they will use their skills to make quick money. If you are skilled with logging equipment and know you can quickly make over $300 from a load of firewood, you might feel it's worth the risk.

Harvesting a Downed Tree

Ideally, if you're heading out to harvest some firewood, you'll want to scout a stormfall tree or a tree that is already on the forest floor. In the woodchopping group I volunteer with, after an intense storm, we often get calls to come collect a tree that has fallen on someone's property. Processing a fallen tree for firewood involves a few steps and may also involve acquiring permission and permits before taking any wood.

It's also a big job to turn a tree into firewood, which means you'll want to call up some friends and neighbors to help. Make sure to have someone on your team who is confident with a chainsaw and has experience with limbing and bucking a downed tree.

First, gather the tools and safety gear you'll need:

Tools:
✓ Chainsaw

✓ Axes (splitting maul and felling axe)

✓ Wedges

Safety Gear:
✓ Work gloves

✓ Safety glasses

✓ Ear protection

✓ Chainsaw chaps

✓ Sturdy boots

Limbing

Bucking

Step 1: Limbing

Use the chainsaw or axe to cut off smaller branches and limbs from the tree trunk. Start from the bottom of the tree and work your way up. Clear the branches out of the way as you go.

Step 2: Bucking

Use a chainsaw to cut the trunk into manageable sections. Typically, the selections are 16 inches (41 cm) in length, which is the ideal size for firewood. It's best to cut from the top down. You'll want to support the trunk as you cut, or it might cave on your chainsaw. Try to put logs and other supports under the trunk to keep it level for cutting.

Step 3: Chopping

Once the trunk has been cut into sections, you can grab your splitting maul and chop the rounds into manageable pieces. Then you can either transport them to another location if needed or continue chopping and stack the wood onsite.

RESPECT

In nature, everything is interconnected. This is central in the traditions of the First Nations. Their cultures reflect a deep-rooted worldview and a unique relationship with the land. While Indigenous cultures across the world are diverse, they share this long-held value.

Traditionally, before cutting down a tree, woodcutters would offer a prayer to honor and thank the tree's spirit for the gift it was about to provide to the community. A respectful understanding of life's cyclical nature.

For Informational Purposes

There is a lot that goes into taking down (felling) a tree. I will preface that I don't want you to think you can go fell a tree after reading this section. There are many dangers to consider with felling. If you need wood for firewood, I guarantee you can find a downed tree that is a deadfall or a tree that was downed from a storm and that will be a lot easier for you to limb, buck, and turn into firewood. This section is just to give you insight into the steps of felling by very experienced people who know what they're doing and are aware of the risks involved.

Today, felling is primarily done with chainsaws, which has sped up the process since the days when it was all done with an axe and crosscut saw. Axes are still used for part of the process to assist the chainsaw though.

The tools and safety gear professionals need:

Tools:

✓ Chainsaw

✓ Wedges

✓ Felling axe

✓ Felling lever

Safety Gear:

✓ Helmet

✓ Eye protection

✓ Ear protection

✓ Gloves

✓ Chainsaw chaps

✓ Sturdy boots

Step 1: Assess the Tree.
A professional examines the tree for any signs of disease, rot, or structural weaknesses. They look for dead branches, cracks, or other hazards.

Step 2: Clear the Area.
A professional surveys the area surrounding the tree to make sure there is nothing hazardous in the tree's fall path or if it can get misdirected during the fall.

Step 3: Plan the Fall.
The professional plans where the tree can fall safely. The natural lean of the tree and the wind direction will help guide the decision.

Step 4: Cut Notches.
Notches are cut into the tree to start influencing the fall. The face (undercut) is the first cut and should be on the side facing the direction you want the tree to fall. There is a top cut at a 70-degree angle, cutting approximately one-third of the way through the tree. Then a horizontal bottom cut is made that meets the top cut. The wedge-shaped piece of wood from the cut is removed.

Step 5: Make the Felling Cut.
The felling cut (also called the back cut) is made on the opposite side of the tree, 1 to 2 inches (2.5 to 5 cm) above the bottom of the face notch. As the back cut is made, wedges are inserted to prevent the tree from leaning back and going off course or restricting the chainsaw from cutting. As the cut continues, the tree will begin to fall—hopefully in the planned fall path.

FROM TREES TO FIREWOOD

The age-old practice of turning a tree into firewood calls for patience, labor, and intention through every stage of the process. It could take weeks to years before wood from the forest reaches its firewood potential. In the end, it'll all pay off when you can look at your firewood piles and feel a strong sense of self-satisfaction and appreciation for this valuable resource.

Hardwood vs. Softwood

Different species of wood have varying properties that affect burning efficiency, heat output, and the amount of smoke produced. Hardwoods, also known as deciduous trees, are generally denser and burn longer than softwoods. These trees shed their leaves in the fall. They usually grow slower than softwoods, which are also known as conifers or evergreens. With the slower growth of hardwoods comes, you guessed it, denser wood, which means a slower burn rate when used as firewood. Hardwoods are preferred for indoor fireplaces and woodstoves for this reason. The grain of softwood trees is less dense, and the wood burns faster. They also tend to produce more smoke than hardwoods. Because softwoods burn fast and catch fast, they are great when used for kindling and for outdoor fires.

When planning on sourcing and collecting firewood, it's ideal to have at least two or three different species of wood in your woodpile.

Having a mixture of wood to burn will help you have more control options for your fire.

THE WOOD IN
MY PILE

My piles change every season and throughout the year, depending on what can be sourced. It's great to have a variety of wood to test out the burning capabilities of different species and be able to have different materials to control your fire temperature. If you want a long night fire, get some dense wood like arbutus, oak, or maple. If you want to heat things up quickly, grab some tinder and a bunch of cedar to bring the heat up fast. The heat will die just as quickly as it started, so you'll have to keep feeding that cedar fire or start adding in some denser wood to hold the heat. This year's pile has three primary wood types.

Western Red Cedar

I love cedar as kindling. It's the quickest wood to catch a flame and very satisfying to chop. Another bonus of cedar is the aroma. It's probably my favorite smell. Sometimes I'll chop up some cedar kindling to bring into the house just for the pleasant scent.

Douglas Fir

The forest in my area has a lot of Douglas fir available. It's a wood that is easy to catch fire but also keeps the heat longer than most softwoods due to its density. Overall, it's one of my most reliable firewoods.

Arbutus

At night, you don't want to get up to throw another log on the fire every hour. If we were only using softwoods like Douglas fir and western red cedar as firewood, then that would be the case. Having some woods that burn longer and at a lower heat is key to staying cozy at night. Thankfully, arbutus is a great night log and can keep the heat going for a long time so we don't have

to get out of bed on cold winter nights to reload the fire.

We also have some miscellaneous piles of wood left from a previous season and small portions sourced from various places. I'm not even sure what some of the wood in the pile is or how it got there, but if it'll burn, I welcome it.

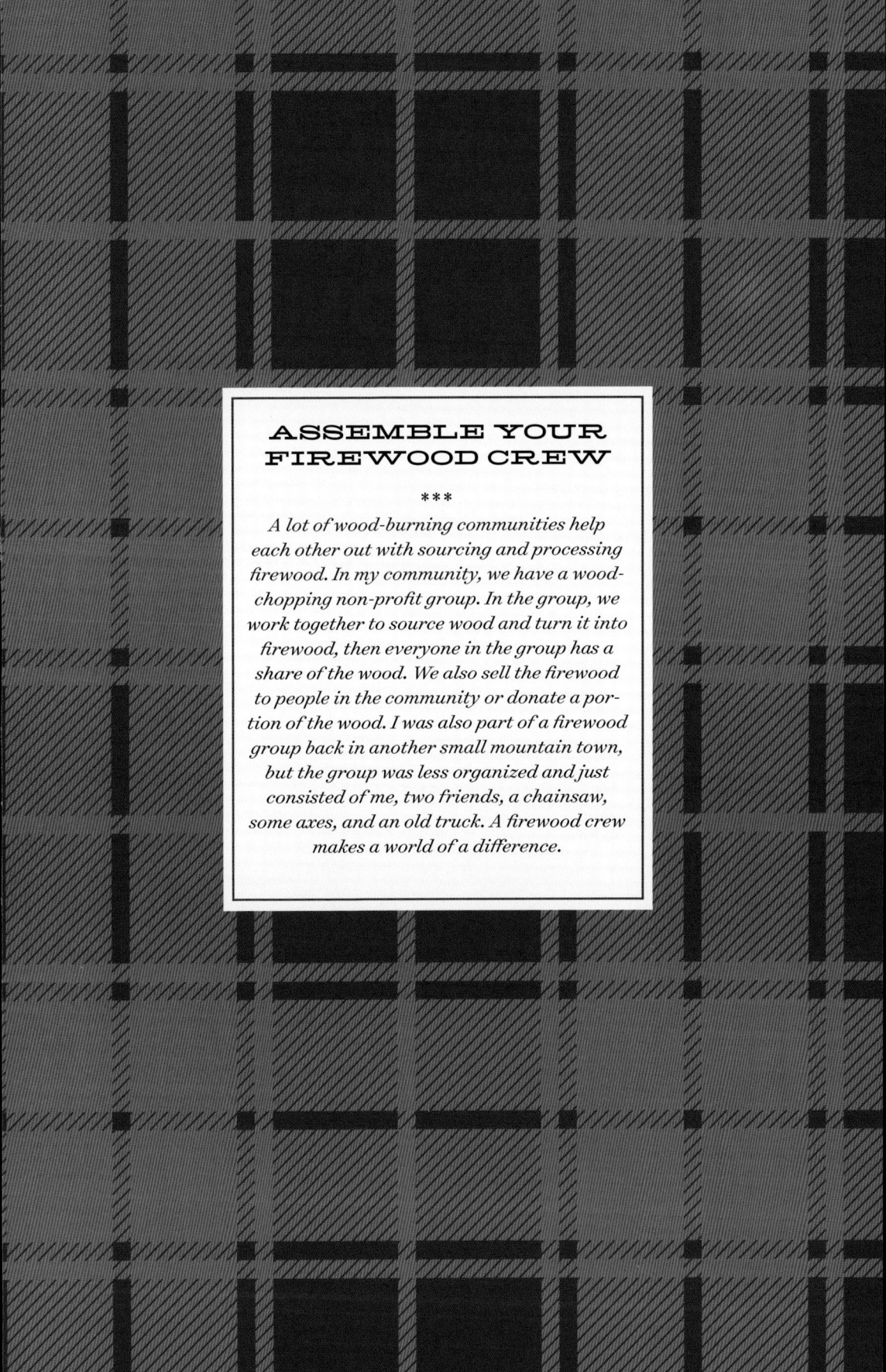

ASSEMBLE YOUR FIREWOOD CREW

***

A lot of wood-burning communities help each other out with sourcing and processing firewood. In my community, we have a wood-chopping non-profit group. In the group, we work together to source wood and turn it into firewood, then everyone in the group has a share of the wood. We also sell the firewood to people in the community or donate a portion of the wood. I was also part of a firewood group back in another small mountain town, but the group was less organized and just consisted of me, two friends, a chainsaw, some axes, and an old truck. A firewood crew makes a world of a difference.

CHAPTER 5

ALL ABOUT FIREWOOD

People take pride in their firewood. If you visit someone's home, especially if it is heated with wood, watch their face light up when they show you their woodpile. They might also mention some stories about the gathering process, something like: "My neighbor came to help me buck and chop up the tree that fell in my yard during the ice storm last winter and now we are set for next winter with all this wood," or maybe, "My friend has a Free Use Permit (FUP) for firewood and had a lot from her last harvest, so I bought a cord off of her."

There is almost always a firewood story, which is something that makes this whole process more unique. Each step, from sourcing wood to stacking to burning, brings an opportunity for connection. Connection with friends and community who help you out or connection with nature that is providing the resource.

In my town, when someone is going through hard times, like the recent death of a spouse, the community comes together to help that person by providing heat for their home. Someone in the community will source the wood and then a crew will go to limb the tree, buck the tree, and chop it into firewood. Then we help stack the wood at the person's home. There is something for everyone to do in this process. It's a small act of hands-on action (or "axe-tion") that brings the community together and warms the home of someone who is missing the warmth of a loved one.

IN THIS CHAPTER

STACKING AND STORING WOOD

There are countless ways to stack firewood. No joke, the Norwegians made a whole art form of it. I highly suggest doing an online search of "Norwegian wood stacks" for some organizational satisfaction, especially if you have a type-A brain. (Think you couldn't stack your woodpile into the shape of a squirrel? You'd be wrong.)

You can really make your wood stack a beautiful backyard masterpiece. But before you fall into the rabbit hole of artful wood stacking and decide your new life's purpose is to run away to Norway and become a wood-stacking artist, let's cover some of the building blocks.

Know the Basics

Stacking and storing wood is an art form, and you'll find there are many options. Don't get overwhelmed. At its heart, here's what to keep in mind.

1. The main goal is to keep your wood away from the ground and protect it from anything that might fall from the sky (rain, snow, or cats and dogs).

2. A secondary goal is to hasten the seasoning process. Proper airflow helps keep moisture from rotting your wood and expedites seasoning. Wood can take from a few months to two years to season, but that's going to depend on how you store it and the environmental conditions it encounters. Keep in mind that hardwoods such as maple, oak, and ash take longer to dry than softwoods like cedar, pine, and spruce.

3. Typically, firewood is cut around 16 inches (41 cm) in length. That is the length that works best for most woodstoves. Keep that in mind if you're designing a space to stack your wood.

Dry It, Season It, Burn It

The primary purpose of storing and stacking wood is to dry it out and get it ready for burning. Through proper methods, you will take "wet wood" (wood that has a high moisture content, likely because it's been freshly felled) and turn it into "seasoned wood" (wood that is dry enough and has been stored properly to make good firewood). The terms *drying* and *seasoning* are often used interchangeably and both terms aim to reduce the moisture content in the wood, but drying firewood is only *a part* of the process of seasoning. Seasoning firewood has a bit more intention behind it. When you've chopped up your firewood and are ready to start setting it up for seasoning, you need to ensure the conditions are ideal for the firewood to reach its burning potential. On the other hand, if you just want to it dry it out, you might leave the wood there and hope the sun hits it for long enough.

Generally, wood needs to dry out for at least six months to two years for it to be ready for burning. A general rule is that if you want to use wood for the winter, you need to let it season for a least one full summer. The summer months are when most of the seasoning happens as heat and sun are needed to start evaporating the water content in

Burning seasoned wood will increase efficiency and decrease creosote buildup.

the wood. The conditions of the wood-pile storage will have a major influence on the seasoning process—we'll explore some of the conditions below. Additionally, different types of wood will have different lengths of seasoning requirements. Conifers (softwoods) such as pine will need a bit longer to season as they typically have more water content compared to deciduous (hardwoods) like oak. We'll be exploring more of these

factors and the right type of burning wood in chapter 6.

Before stacking your woodpile, find an area in your yard that has dry ground with good drainage. If you happen to live on the West Coast, like myself, and dry ground is harder to come by, no problem; there is always a way to make things work. The solution here is to be more diligent about creating a platform to elevate the woodpile.

Airflow

Air is important in the process of seasoning wood. As air circulates around the wood, it carries away the moisture that has evaporated from the wood fibers. This promotes the drying process by removing the water vapor from the wood. Encouraging airflow helps prevent the growth of mold and fungi, which thrive in damp conditions, and proper ventilation ensures that the wood dries uniformly. If one side of the wood has poor ventilation, it may dry at a different rate than the other sections. Efficient airflow accelerates the drying process. When moist air is continuously replaced with drier air, the moisture gradient between the wood and the surrounding air is maintained, promoting faster water migration out of the wood. Having adequate airflow will prevent case hardening, which is when the outer layers of wood dry faster than the inner layer. This creates a shell that makes it harder for further moisture to evaporate. Proper airflow helps prevent case hardening by causing moisture to escape evenly from the wood.

To set up piles with good airflow, think of the environment the stack will be in and how tightly you'll be stacking the pieces. You want the stack to be tight enough to keep the pile secure but loose enough to let a good breeze flow through. As your wood dries out, the pieces will shrink and the pile will shift a bit. Take that shifting as a positive sign of your wood becoming seasoned.

Proper airflow around the stacked wood ensures it stays dry and ready for effective burning.

Pests

Piles of wood can attract a variety of pests that can cause problems for both the wood itself and your home. Before bringing in wood from the stacks outside, I give the pieces a hard drop on the ground to hopefully shake off any spiders that might be lurking in the pile. Some pests are relatively harm-less, including the spiders that give more of a scare factor than a major threat. But some pests like carpenter ants and termites will be hazardous if they start occupying your woodpile and, if you don't catch them, eventually your home. Here are some common firewood pile pests.

PEST	SIGNS
Termites: Small, wood-eating insects that can cause significant damage to wooden structures.	Mud tubes, hollow-sounding wood, and discarded wings.
Carpenter Ants: Large black or red ants that tunnel through wood to create nests.	Sawdust piles near the woodpile, rustling sounds inside the wood.
Spiders: There are many different types of spiders that may be attracted to your woodpile. Most are harmless, but depending on what's in your region, you might attract some venomous spiders.	Webs in and around the woodpile.
Rodents: Mice, rats, and other small mammals might like to make homes in firewood piles.	Droppings, claw marks, nests.
Wasps and Hornets: Hopefully you'll notice these before they get too serious. They'll take over the area by creating a nest near the woodpile.	Nests, buzzing sounds, sightings of wasps or hornets.

The best ways to deal with unwanted visitors are prevention, maintenance, and inspection. Prevention takes prepa-ration. Properly storing wood off the ground and away from conditions that keep it damp helps deter most insects. Insects and a lot of other pests are not as interested in invading woodpiles of really dry, seasoned wood. Follow the guides above for proper wood storage and it will also help prevent woodpile conditions that attract pests. Another tip for prevention is to keep your woodpiles away from your home. If you start seeing signs of harmful pests like carpenter ants in your woodpile and your woodpile is stacked right against your home, you're going to need to double your concern. If your woodpile is at least a few feet from your home or any buildings, you'll have more of a chance to isolate the pest issue.

To prevent the jump scare of finding a spider or unwanted guest on your little fireside indoor woodpile, keep your indoor woodpile small. Only bring in the wood you plan to use immediately to minimize the chance of pests entering your home. You can also do the classic method of dropping the wood pieces onto the ground to shake off any potential hidden pests before bringing the wood inside.

Maintenance of the woodpile is also important. Mice and small mammals will build nests in messy woodpiles. If your woodpile has a lot of wood chips and forest debris around it, those items will make great material for a little mouse family to start settling in. Keep your woodpiles maintained to keep unwanted visitors out. If you do come across some woodpile residents, be humane in how you handle their eviction. They use this natural resource to make a cozy home, just like you.

You can also invite natural predators to help with woodpile watch. Birds do a great job at managing some little pests. Place a bird feeder close to your pile to attract natural predators to keep the unwanted pests out.

Regularly inspect your woodpile for the presence of pests and manage them early, before they become problematic.

A Buyer's Guide to Woodsheds

If you're in the market for a proper woodshed, here's a buyer's guide of what to look for.

There are several key factors to think about before buying a woodshed, and the same is true if you plan to build your own woodshed.

Size: Assess how much firewood you need to store. Consider your average usage and ensure the shed can accommodate enough wood to last through at least a season.

Dimensions: Ensure the shed has enough space to stack wood properly, allowing for airflow and easy access.

Materials: Common materials include:
1. Wood: Provides a natural look but requires regular maintenance.
2. Metal: Durable and low maintenance, but may be prone to rust if not treated.
3. Plastic/Vinyl: Weather-resistant and low maintenance, but might not be as sturdy as wood or metal.

Foundation: A solid foundation, such as concrete or treated wood, will prevent the shed from sinking or shifting and keep the wood off the ground, reducing moisture exposure.

Ease of Use: Ensure the shed has wide doors or openings for easy loading and unloading of firewood. Consider the height and accessibility for comfortable stacking and retrieval.

Placement: Choose a location that is convenient for accessing firewood, close to your home or the area where you use

the wood. Avoid low-lying areas prone to flooding.

Sun Exposure: Placing the shed in a sunny spot can help promote faster drying and reduce moisture.

Price: Consider your budget and the cost of the shed. Higher-quality materials and larger sizes will generally cost more but can provide better durability and protection for your firewood.

DIY vs. Prebuilt: DIY projects can be more cost effective and customizable but require time and skill. If you're building your own shed, you can make it just the way you want it. If you want to put up shelves, add that to your DIY blueprints and make them the height that suits your needs. When buying a shed, prioritize size, materials, ventilation, and weather protection to ensure your firewood stays dry and accessible. By considering these factors, you can select or build a woodshed that effectively meets your needs and enhances your property.

No Woodshed? No Problem.

As I've mentioned, you want to make sure you keep your wood off the ground to prevent it from gaining moisture and rotting. If you don't have a perfectly designed and ready-to-use woodshed, you can keep your wood off the ground by using a few long logs as planks to elevate your pile by a few inches. Or maybe you have some old wood pallets you can put to use. If not, your local recycling depot might have some old pallets available. Once your wood has something to protect it from the ground, you also want to protect it from above.

Use whatever you have available to store your wood.

You're going to provide shelter to keep it away from rain and snow. For quick top protection, you can use tarps. However, tarps don't always allow for good airflow, which means the moisture might be retained and the wood will take longer to dry out or could start rotting.

After a long session of woodchopping, you may not have the energy to stack right away. A tarp can be used as temporary shelter to protect your pile until you've rested up and are ready to stack. If you are stacking your wood between two trees, you'll have a bit of top shelter from the leaves and branches. Keep in mind that even evergreens will shed their foliage, so the top layer of your stack might develop a layer of leaves, twigs, and branches over time. Also, the debris from the trees might add moisture to the top layer of the stack. This again highlights why it is so important to have a layer of top protection to keep the drying process chugging along.

Remember that a shelter needs to last for at least a couple of months to a few years, or as long as you'll be using wood as a heat source, so take some time to develop methods that use your space effectively and set up your woodpiles to season with ease. A lot of methods of self-sufficiency, such as gardening, farming, canning, or using firewood, do require some extra time to set up the operation and hone your approach to the process. Depending on your circumstances and the resources available, you may need to expedite some of the steps, such as providing a temporary shelter. But overall, the more work you can put in up front, the more success you'll have with the outcome. So, if you don't have a woodshed in the beginning, don't worry. You can still create a seasoning environment for your wood and consider better structures in the future.

Stacking Patterns

An age-old debate with stacking is whether you should have the bark side up or face down. Personally, I find bark side up helps avoid additional moisture retention, but I live on the West Coast, so we have a bit more humidity to deal with. Now on to the various patterns you can use.

Row on Row

The most common stacking pattern is to stack your wood row on row, with the wood pieces in rows and the rows on top of each other in the same direction, with the cut ends facing outward. If you're using this pattern, you'll need "bookends" to keep your rows in place because this stack won't be able to stand alone. This is where a stacking rack can come in handy. You can also use some natural spaces by stacking your rows between two trees for support. If you don't have natural structures, you can do a log cabin pattern at the end of your row to hold it in place.

Log Cabin

The log cabin stacking pattern is a great technique to keep your row-on-row stack in place or you can use a few of the log cabin pillars to create a freestanding pile. To build a log cabin:

1. Stack three pieces of cut wood beside each other in the same direction and then stack three pieces on top and perpendicular to that layer. It will look exactly like the wood bricks in the game Jenga. However, I recommend trying to avoid the temptation to start removing the lower wood pieces to balance them on top and see how high you can get (unless you're bored and really like stacking wood repeatedly).

2. Continue the rows upward, making sure each layer is sturdy before placing more on top. Stop when they begin to feel unstable (you don't want to actually play Jenga). Start building your next stack beside the first one.

When you're ready to use the wood, you'll start taking logs from the top layers and work your way down. Over time, some of the most nicely stacked log cabin piles can start to take on more of a row-on-row organization.

Add a little style to your stack.

Beehive

The beehive stacking pattern, also known as the wood house or *holz hausen* (German for "wood house"), is another traditional pattern that creates effective airflow and is aesthetically pleasing.

1. Begin the beehive by laying wood pieces in a circle, making sure the wood is angled slightly, with its outer ends higher than its inner ends. This will help with stability. Continue stacking circular rows with the ends slightly up. As the stack grows the slight angle will help create the beehive shape.

2. Keep the center hollow to allow airflow.

3. You can also cap the top by roofing it with pieces of bark.

MISFITS

Let's talk about misfits. If you've worked with other resources directly from nature, you might know by now that some things can't be made into perfect shapes; that's also part of nature's beauty. Therefore, you'll probably have some wood pieces that are very irregular with knots sticking out or with very twisted grain. You'll probably also have some pieces that are longer and shorter, all different shapes and sizes. These misfit pieces will be harder to put into a uniform stack. You can keep these in a separate pile or play a bit of Tetris and find places for these pieces in your main stack. Some wood species will also inevitably be in odd shapes. When you chop arbutus wood, it rarely chops in a straight-grain, uniform way. Each chopped piece is its own unique shape and usually has multiple colors like maroon, yellow, and sometimes purple. Each wood piece almost looks like a work of art. Arbutus is a great wood for burning because it burns long and strong, but trying to stack arbutus will take some creativity to pile the wood and allow airflow. I've seen some people use the outer grates from water storage tanks as a container for their misfit firewood stacks. At the end of the day, if the wood is burnable, we're going to keep it no matter what it looks like. Thankfully, there are always ways to figure out how to give your woodpile what it needs to season it for burning.

HOW TO TELL WHEN WOOD IS SEASONED

You've stacked it properly. You've stored it properly. Now you can use the wood, right? Or does it need to season longer? Let's explore.

Eyes and Ears

Although it takes a long time for wood to dry out, there are a few indicators to help you gauge your progress. You'll want to check for changes in color, grain, and weight. With some exceptions to this rule, typically wood will become lighter in color as it seasons. So, keep an eye on the tone change. If the wood was vibrant with multiple color hues when it was first chopped, during the seasoning process the colors will become dull and fade as the wood loses its moisture content. Typically, the wood will also develop a slight gray tone.

You will also likely see changes in the grain, such as cracking and small openings on the cut side. This happens due to the moisture leaving the wood. As the wood loses its water weight, it will also become lighter. Softwoods like cedar have a very high moisture content when they are freshly cut, so when they dry out, the weight difference is noticeable.

You can also hear the difference between wet wood and dry from the sound. If you're chopping wet wood, it's going to have a lower, dull sound due to the moisture density, as opposed to dry wood, which will have a high-pitch crack when you chop.

Moisture Meter

If you want to get really accurate with knowing the moisture content of your wood, you can use a moisture meter. Moisture meters typically work by using probes or sensors that are inserted into the wood. A lot of moisture meters will have different modes for reading soft-wood or hardwood. The device then provides a reading indicating the percentage of moisture present. Are you sick of the word *moisture* yet?

Soap Test

Let's take ourselves back to a fun day in grade-school science class by doing the good ol' soap test. This test will help us determine whether our wood is properly seasoned and ready to burn.

To start, grab some dish soap and a piece of wood from your stack. Next, rub some soapy water on one side of the wood. Then, see if you can blow through the dry side to make bubbles appear on the soapy side. If you can, your wood is dry!

Next, let's take a look at the art and craft of fire building.

If you pay attention to your stack, you'll notice the changes in color, sound, and weight.

WOOD BURNING BTU

(BRITISH THERMAL UNITS)

***

Wood burning BTU (British Thermal Units) is a way of measuring the amount of energy released or heat output by wood as it burns. In firewood, BTUs measure the heat output or energy content of the wood. Higher BTU means more heat output and greater efficiency in heating. The BTU value of wood can vary widely depending on the type of wood, its moisture content, and how it is processed. Hardwoods like oak or hickory can produce around 20 million to 30 million BTU per cord. Softwoods like pine or fir typically produce less heat, around 15 million to 25 million BTU per cord.

CHAPTER 6

BUILDING FIRES

There is nothing like sitting around a campfire on a summer night, sharing the warmth and light with friends, hearing the rhythmic crackling of the fire and being surrounded by the ambience of nocturnal nature. Campfires have such a rich association with celebrations, gatherings, and sharing. There is something ingrained in our DNA that when we see, smell, or hear a campfire, we are attracted to it like bugs to a lamp.

I'm sure we all have memories of being around a campfire at some point in our lives. It's where we learned to roast marshmallows and inevitably burned a few in the process (sometimes intentionally). It's a place for storytelling, whether you're telling ghost stories with new friends at summer camp or sharing personal journeys on a hiking trip with old friends. Creating a campfire is creating a space for connection. But in order to have a fire, you need the proper elements.

ELEMENTS OF A FIRE

A fire is the result of a chemical reaction known as combustion. Combustion occurs through the combination of three elements: heat, fuel, and oxygen. Together, these three elements are referred to as the "fire triangle." There are also three phases to combustion.

1. Pre-Ignition: This involves drying and removing the water content in front of the fuel to get it ready. This is when you have tinder, kindling, and seasoned fuelwood ready to heat up. All the elements are prepared to create the combustion reaction.

2. Flaming Combustion: You've ignited the tinder, which is now producing gases from the ignition, and you can see visible flames. The flame then catches onto the kindling and eventually the fuelwood as it builds.

3. Smoldering Combustion: This is when the flames have died down and the heat has lowered but there is still a slow burn on the fuel that continues without a flame. This is where you'll see the glowing embers.

Heat + Fuel + Oxygen = Combustion

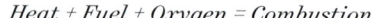

Where the magic happens

BUILDING A FIRE

Building a fire is more than just laying some sticks on the ground and igniting them. There is a method to the madness. You'll have to think about the area, materials, and maintenance, as well as the weather and environment.

Prepare the Firepit

Before we spark some flames, we are going to ensure we have a good area for building a fire. Clear a space for the fire, then take a step back and confirm the area is free from anything that could catch fire. Dig away 2 inches (5 cm) of dirt to get right to the bare ground. You can also add a rock wall ring around your pit to help contain the fire. A little safety note for the rocks: Don't collect any rocks from a river or other body of water because they could explode with the heat of the fire. Collect your rocks from a dry area away from wetlands. Once you're confident with your firepit, let's heat things up! There are three different materials and wood cuts used to make most fires.

Tinder

To get a fire going, first gather your materials. Let's start with some tinder. Tinder is any material that lights easily and burns quickly. It provides the initial heat needed to get the bigger pieces going. Here are some ideas for tinder.

Dry Grass: Make sure it's extra dry and straw-like. The drier the grass, the better the burn.

Brown Paper and Newspaper: Save up your brown paper grocery bags and newspapers because they make excellent fire starters. You can also use them as a wrap for other tinder: put some dry bark and grass in a paper bag, roll it up, and the tinder package you just made will amplify your spark.

Dryer Lint: Yes, dryer lint will light up quickly. Better yet, mix in some dog or cat hair and you'll have a flame going in no time.

Twine: Have some leftover twine rope from gardening or other backyard projects? You can tie up some dry grass or brown paper pieces to spark up and get your fire started.

As you may know, things may catch fire, which offers a lot of options for tinder. You can use materials from the forest floor or from inside your home. Spark it up!

The oils in birch bark will help spark up a flame even in wet weather.

Dry Bark: Bark from a cedar tree is very fibrous and almost stringy, so it will ignite like twine and brown paper once it's dried out. Bark from a paper birch tree is one of the best tinder materials when you're scavenging for fire starters in the forest.

There are hundreds of things you can use for tinder. You can find a lot of natural tinder in the forest or scout some safe flammables in your recycling bin. Be careful to avoid anything with toxic fumes or dangerous chemicals. I suggest sticking to natural materials for a clear burn.

My Approach: The Tinder Bundle
With so many materials able to be scouted and sourced, I usually try to make a tinder bundle with what's available.

CREATE A LINT LOG

Here's a great little fire starter you can make using things in your home. Grab an empty toilet paper roll. Gather some lint from the dryer. If you don't have dryer lint, do you have a furry animal? Collect some dog or cat hair for the job. Put the lint and/or fur into the roll. You can add some paper towel or scrap paper to stuff the roll a bit more. If you want to add a little extra, pour some melted wax into the roll. The wax will help it burn a bit longer.

Similarly, you can use an empty egg carton. Put some lint, paper, or dry grass in the egg pods and pour on some wax. Let the wax dry and you have convenient little fire-starting pods. When you've got your fire set and ready to burn, light up a lint log or an egg carton pod to get things sparking.

First, I'll grab very dry cedar bark, which I like using because it's widely available in my backyard firewood piles and it's very easy to peel into string-like strips for the tinder bundle. I'll also grab a handful of wood chips from the cleanup pile in the yard, just as long as the chips are dry enough. I usually have a pile of brown paper bags from grocery shopping trips I save for burning. Another thing I usually have on hand is twine, which I use to bundle the materials together.

To bundle, I tear the paper bags into smaller sections, brush a light layer of Vaseline on the paper, then place the gathered tinder materials on the paper. You don't want your materials to look nice and neat; you want it to look like messy tumbleweed. Then, roll up the paper with the materials inside and use the twine to rope it together. You don't need to pack it tightly because having a bit of room in the bundle will make it

catch faster. I usually use this for starting a fire in my woodstove. I place the bundle in the center of the firebox and create a little kindling teepee over the bundle. Once the kindling is in place, I'll set the bundle on fire and watch as the flames begin moving to catch the kindling.

Kindling

Kindling is typically added to the fire after the tinder has ignited, helping to build and maintain the flames until larger pieces of wood can catch fire. Kindling usually refers to thin pieces of dry wood that you can place in your fire to help flames catch onto the wood. It helps bring more heat to the fire and transition thev fire onto the bigger firewood pieces. I find dry pieces of cedar and other quick-burning softwoods great to use as kindling. Generally, you'll want to use softwoods for kindling and hardwoods for fuel logs.

Firewood/Fuel Logs

Now it's time to grab some firewood. Grab wood of various thickness, from two fingers thin to an arm or a leg thick. It's always best to grab more than you think you'll need. Hardwoods that are slow burning, such as hickory, oak, and elm, are ideal to keep your fire burning long and strong. If hardwoods aren't available, then you'll need to feed the fire a bit more often, so grab lots of whatever is available.

Feather out the end of a stick or piece of wood to help a flame catch.

CAMPFIRE STRUCTURES

Different types of campfires serve different purposes and have unique characteristics. Here are some common types.

Teepee Fire
In this traditional campfire style, small and long pieces of wood are arranged in a cone shape. It's excellent for quickly generating heat and light, and is ideal for cooking and providing warmth. This is one of the easiest fires to assemble and get going.

Step 1: Gather some kindling, ideally items similar in length.

Step 2: Place your tinder in the center of the pit.

Step 3: Lean the kindling against each other to build a cone shape over the tinder.

Step 4: Ignite the tinder inside the teepee.

Step 5: Once the flame starts building you can add fuelwood outside of the structure to keep the fire going.

Log Cabin Fire

The log cabin layout involves placing wood pieces in a square frame and stacking them on top. Place smaller pieces of tinder inside for the flame. This will burn with a steady heat and is great for long-lasting cooking fires.

Step 1: Gather some pieces of wood, with a slight variety of sizes.

Step 2: Place your tinder in the center of the pit.

Step 3: Lay two parallel pieces of fuelwood on opposite sides of the tinder pile. Place two more pieces of fuelwood perpendicular to the first two, forming a square or rectangle around the tinder. This forms the first "log cabin" layer.

Step 4: Repeat this layering, alternating directions, and start using smaller pieces of wood as you build up.

Step 5: Ignite the tinder in the log cabin.

Step 6: Add more fuelwood outside of the log cabin or across the top to maintain the fire.

Log cabin layout: Slow burn and great for cooking

Lean-to Fire

In a lean-to fire, one log is placed horizontally on the ground, and smaller pieces of wood are leaned against it at an angle, creating a sheltered space where the fire can burn. It's useful in windy conditions and can provide a consistent flame.

Step 1: Lay a large log or place a big rock on the ground on the windward side of your firepit. This will act as a windbreak and provide support for your lean-to structure.

Step 2: Place a small pile of tinder on the ground next to the windbreak log or rock. Lean thin pieces of kindling against the windbreak in a way that shelters the tinder.

Step 3: Ignite the tinder.

Step 4: Once the flame starts building, add some thin fuelwood over the flame and keep it protected from the wind.

Lean-to layout: Protects the flame from wind and harsh conditions

Upside-Down Fire

Similar to the log cabin, with this pattern you'll stack layers on top of each other with no spaces in the middle. Make the layers smaller as you build up. Lay your tinder on top of the stack. Light this fire from the top so it will burn down slowly to provide a long heat.

Step 1: Gather various sizes of fuel logs.

Step 2: Lay the largest wood pieces side by side at the bottom of your firepit. Ensure they are packed closely together to form a solid base.

Step 3: Place a layer of slightly smaller logs on top of the base layer, perpendicular to the first layer. This crisscross pattern helps with stability and airflow.

Step 4: Continue adding layers of increasingly smaller wood pieces, alternating the direction of each row.

Step 5: Once you've got to the smallest layer, place a pile of tinder on top of the structure and start the flame.

Upside-down layout: Provides a very long burn

Star Fire

This method involves arranging logs and branches in a star-like pattern around a central point, leaving gaps between them for air circulation. It's effective for creating a long-lasting, low flame and can be useful for signaling or cooking.

Step 1: Create a pile of tinder in the center of your firepit.

Step 2: Place kindling around the tinder pile, forming a small teepee or a loose pile.

Step 3: Take five long fuelwood pieces and arrange them in a star pattern around the tinder and kindling pile. Each long wood piece should meet the tinder pile at its center.

Step 4: Ignite the tinder pile. You can bring the fuelwood closer to the center to burn quicker or make them more distant to help the fire last longer.

Step 5: Add more fuelwood to the star pattern to keep the fire alive.

Star layout: This simple layout doesn't require a lot to keep the flame alive (unlike your ex).

Swedish Log/Canadian Candle

Here's one that's a little different—the Swedish log fire, also known as the Canadian candle. This fire layout is just a single-log fire. It's efficient because you just need one log and it provides a surface for cooking.

Step 1: Grab a log that is 12 to 15 inches (31 to 38 cm) in width.

Step 2: Split the log in quarters most of the way vertically and leave the bottom attached, so your cuts create an opening.

Step 3: Place tinder in the openings of your log.

Step 4: As the fire starts to burn down the log, feed the flame with tinder and kindling as needed.

This method offers a lot of simplicity, extended burn time, and versatility in cooking.

MAINTAINING A FIRE

Once you decide what kind of fire pattern you want and what materials you have, it's time to start arranging your wood in your chosen fire pattern. Remember to keep your kindling and fuelwood for feeding the fire close by. Your fire is like your childhood goldfish: if you want to keep it alive, you need to remember to feed it. As the fire catches and the kindling begins to burn, gradually add larger pieces of fuelwood to sustain the fire. Be mindful not to smother the flames. Lastly, keep an eye on the fire and add more fuelwood as needed to maintain the desired size and intensity.

EXTINGUISHING A FIRE

As mentioned above, there are three things a fire needs: heat, fuel, and oxygen. Combined, these the elements will get a fire started and keep it going. Removing any one of these elements can stop the combustion process and extinguish the fire. If you take away the fire's oxygen supply by smothering it in a fire blanket, it'll die. Similarly, if you take away its fuel, the combustion won't sustain.

Once you're done with your fire, allow the flames to burn down to the ash before extinguishing it. This will reduce access to fuel. Once the flames are out, break up and spread out the embers. This helps cool them down. To extinguish a campfire, use the drowning method. Grab large quantities of water and douse the wood fuel, embers, and ashes until the hissing sound stops, starting from the edges of the firepit and working toward the center. Make sure everything in the pit is wet, even the embers that weren't red with heat. Heat tends to hide inside some materials, so make sure you've thoroughly soaked the firepit. Next, stir the pile to ensure everything is wet and spread out the materials from the hot firepit center. Then, get some soil or sand and add it to the now-wet firepit mix. Continue by mixing the dirt, sand, and water into the firepit until everything is completely cooled. If anything in the firepit is too hot to touch, it's too hot to leave. Ensure the fire is fully extinguished before leaving the site.

Keep in mind that even if the flame is gone, combustion may still be happening. The embers and ashes from a fire will still hold heat for a long while after the flame is out. Also keep in mind that not all fires are the same. We are focusing on wood fires for this book. Extinguishing an oil fire or electrical fire will be very different methods of extinguishing.

WOOD ASH IN
THE GARDEN

Did you know that wood ash can be great for your garden? The ash contains a variety of nutrients that fertilize the soil and assist in plant growth. These nutrients include potassium, calcium, and magnesium as well as trace minerals such as sulfur, zinc, iron, manganese, and copper. These minerals are released into the ash as the wood is burning and remain in the ash after burning. You can evenly distribute small amounts around fruit trees or mix it in throughout your garden bed. One thing to keep in mind is that wood ash has a high pH level. You can test your soil to determine whether more alkalinity is needed before you introduce ash to your soil.

Adding small amounts of wood ash to a compost pile can also help add nutrients to your mix and speed up the composting process. Aim for a maximum of 5 percent of your compost pile's volume to keep things balanced.

COOKING WITH FIRE

Nothing is better than enjoying a delicious meal made over an open fire. It creates memorable culinary experiences in the great outdoors. I remember going to one of my first overnight Girl Guide camps. We spent the evening around the fire making campfire wraps. We each filled our wraps with our chosen ingredients, like veggies, lettuce, ground beef, and cheese. Then we each wrapped our creations in tinfoil and placed them in the firepit. We quickly learned that putting them too close to the flame would char the wrap, which led to some casualties. By the second round of cooking, all the wraps were piled in the prime spot on the red embers to cook more evenly. For dessert, we had some classic campfire s'mores.

You can't really have a group campfire without s'mores. All experienced s'more makers seem to develop their own technique. Some like to stick their marshmallow right into the hot flame and let the outer layer char and burn off, creating an extra gooey, sticky glob. Some like to find the lower heat areas of the fire and keep a consistent rotation of their stick to produce an even, golden-brown coating around their marshmallow like a true s'more artisan. One of the fun parts about making campfire snacks is being able to make mistakes and get creative. Even if you burn your marshmallow right off your stick, just grab another one from the bag and try again. The experience of cooking with fire and the process of learning and sharing with friends creates a delicious treat, no matter how your food turns out.

GET CREATIVE WITH S'MORES!

A classic s'more recipe is two graham crackers sandwiching a piece of melted chocolate with a gooey, fire-heated marshmallow to create a soft and crunchy treat. Once you know the basics and have mastered your marshmallow heating, you can get creative and add some new ingredients to this classic recipe. Maybe try adding some fire-roasted banana pieces or other types of fruit like strawberries. For a peanut butter twist, use peanut butter cups instead of chocolate, or spread some peanut butter on your graham crackers. Maybe sprinkle some cinnamon on the marshmallow for a bit of spice. Want to try a s'more bowl? Instead of graham crackers, pile some gooey marshmallows in a waffle cone and add your favorite ice-cream toppings like sprinkles and chocolate chips.

The Best Woods for Campfire Cooking

Like pairing a fine wine with your meal, choosing the right type of wood for your campfire cooking will influence the flavor and outcome of your meal. The most distinctive contribution of cooking with fire is the smoky flavor it brings. This happens because when wood burns, the compounds produced from the burning attach to the surface of the food as it's heating up, creating the smoke flavor. Cooking with direct heat over wood is also great for caramelizing food with sugars, like fruits and vegetables. The sugars in food will cook into a sweet, butter-like flavor at the high temperatures produced through campfire cooking.

If you're looking to get a fire going with the purpose of cooking, remember that you'll want a fire where you can maintain a consistent heat level, such as a log cabin layout. Make sure you have plenty of fuel to keep the fire going strong and your food cooking. Rotating or stirring the food frequently will also ensure an even cook.

Here are some great choices for cooking firewood and their characteristics.

If you know your softwoods (conifers) from your hardwoods (deciduous) trees, you might notice the choices I shared here are all hardwoods. Hardwoods tend to produce less smoke because they have little to no resin. Softwoods contain resin, which will turn to smoke while burning. Hardwoods also burn longer and keep a more consistent heat, which is ideal for cooking food. Hardwood also tends to produce a cleaner burn, meaning you're not as likely to have rogue embers shooting onto your food.

	USE WITH	CHARACTERISTISCS	FLAVOR
Oak	Great for grilling meats and slow cooking	Dense, burns long and steadily	Mildly smoky and sweet
Hickory	Grilling and smoking meats such as pork, beef, and chicken	Burns hot and long	Strong, smoky, bacon-like
Maple	Vegetables and meats; great for all foods	Burns hot and clean	Mildly sweet and smoky
Birch	Quick grilling of meats and vegetables	Burns quickly and hot	Mild and sweet

KINDLE YOUR SKILLS

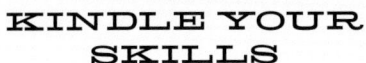

When you burn wood for heat, you inevitably spend a lot of time around it. You'll put in many hours harvesting wood, chopping wood, storing wood, staring lovingly at your wood pile, and so on. The more time you spend around firewood, the more you'll be able to notice the differences of the wood in your area. The different densities of the grain, the ease of chopping, the smells, the looks of the bark, etc. You'll also become a more efficient firestarter when you have to cut your own kindling and rely on your wood-seasoning ability to provide warmth. The more you work with firewood, the more skills you'll gain to help your firewood work better with you.

CONCLUSION

As our journey through blades, wood, and fire draws to a close, I hope this book has kindled your passion for the forest and the timeless crafts that thrive within it. We've explored the history of how axes shaped our world, the thrill of chopping wood, the duties of properly caring for your firewood, and the art of building a good campfire for you and your loved ones to enjoy. Beyond the practical skills and techniques, we've delved into the spirit of self-sufficiency and the deep satisfaction of living more simply in connection with nature. Each moment spent with your axe in hand will remind you of the simple joys and enduring traditions that define the human experience.

If you want to continue your journey down the road of blades, wood, and fire, here are a few paths you can explore with your knowledge and skills:

Blacksmithing: Learn the traditional craft of forging and shaping metal to create your own axes and blades. Many local blacksmiths run workshops to help you get started.

Logging Sports: A heritage sport derived from the skills loggers would have used in the forest way back when, logging sports involve various disciplines with modern tools, like chainsaw racing, and with tools from the past, such as bucking with a crosscut saw.

Community Groups: If you're a family or community that uses firewood for heat, there is likely an official or unofficial group of nearby people who get together to help each other with firewood tasks. If you're unsure whether a group exists, why not get some people together and start one? Find out what people need help with, whether it's a group that helps with sourcing wood, bucking and chopping wood, or storing and stacking—or perhaps all of it. If you're looking to start a group, you can structure it as a co-op where everyone works together and shares the fruits of the labor. It's always more efficient and enjoyable to do these tasks with others.

Wood Carving: The more comfortable you get with your axe and learn about the various types of woods and their properties, the more you can expand your skill set and get more creative with your woodworking. If you want to see the crafty ways a blade can shape a piece of wood, try picking up a carving axe and shape a wood piece into a spoon.

The above are just a few examples. There are endless possibilities for expansion with the skill sets we've touched on. As you close this book, I hope you continue to sharpen your axe skills and keep the flame of your fire knowledge lit.

RESOURCES

EDUCATION AND COMMUNITY

Arboristsite.com
A site where Arborists and enthusiasts discuss tools, techniques, and all things tree care.

Outdoor Skills Schools
Schools that focus on survival and bushcraft often have courses on axe skills and firewood gathering.

Community Woodlot Associations
Look for local woodlot owners' associations that offer resources and local connections on firewood production and woodlot management.

Your Neighbor
If you live in an area where people use firewood for heat, you're going to be able to find someone who is happy to lend a hand and share their knowledge on the process. The people in your region who will be working with the same climates, regulations, and resources are going to be your best assets for learning what you need to know.

Chainsaw Safety Classes
There are many classes and courses offered by equipment manufacturers like Husqvarna and Stihl, or by local community organizations.

AXE RECOMMENDATIONS

Fiskars X Series
Fiskars has a great line of axes. They are incredibly durable and suitable for anyone who is just starting out or for those who are looking to advance their skill. The Fiskars X27 axe with a 36-inch (91 cm) handle is a great choice for all things firewood.

Gränsfors Bruk
Gränsfors Bruk are hand-forged axes that have been made in Sweden for over 100 years. They offer a variety of high-quality axes for different wood-chopping and bushcraft needs.

Local Blacksmiths
If you value supporting a local artisan, try scouting out a Blacksmith who makes axes. Choosing a hand-forged axe over a mass-produced one has some benefits. The repeated heating, hammering, and tempering process of the metal improves the molecular structure of the material, making hand-forged axes stronger. Not only will there be more attention to detail due to the hands-on process but the axe will also have a rugged beauty, making it a unique piece to your tool collection.

PHOTOGRAPHY CREDITS

Davy Rippner Woodchopper-Emeritus:
page 42

Melanie Orr Photography:
pages 12, 16, 22, 24, 34–37, 43, 44, 47–49, 51,
54–55, 60, 61, 66, 67, 74, 81–85, 87, 88, 92–97,
104–107, 131, 134–137, 151, 153, 162, 174, 188,
198–199

Nicole Coenen:
pages 6, 8, 10, 18, 23, 28–29, 31, 33, 40, 45, 46,
50, 52, 53, 56–59, 62–65, 68–69, 72, 76–79,
86, 89–91, 99–103, 112–125, 138–139, 142,
143, 146, 152, 158–160, 163, 166–173, 175–183,
190–191, 192, 194, 196

Shutterstock:
pages 129, 130, 133, 140–141, 148–149, 156–157,
161, 184

ACKNOWLEDGMENTS

Writing this book on forests, firewood, and axes has been a journey. To be honest, writing a book around these passions was never something I thought I'd have the opportunity to do, and now that it's printed and in your hands, I feel so incredibly grateful to the many individuals and organizations whose support, knowledge, and encouragement have made this work possible.

First and foremost, I extend an acknowledgment to the beautiful land I am grateful to live and work on: the traditional, ancestral, and unceded territory of the Coast Salish Peoples, specifically the lands of the Tsawout First Nation. Located in the Salish Sea, this place has been home to the Tsawout Peoples and other Coast Salish communities for thousands of years. The rich history, culture, and stewardship of these lands by the First Peoples are deeply honored and respected. In acknowledging the traditional caretakers of this land, I recognize the importance of understanding and appreciating the history and contributions of Indigenous Peoples.

I am profoundly grateful to my mentors like Jeri Sparshu from Thistle Rock Forge, who has been a continuous guide through my blacksmithing journey. Thanks for trusting me to come to your workspace to play with metal and fire to make blades; your bravery is appreciated. Thanks to my logging sports coach Ben James, whose enthusiasm and passion for all things lumberjack has been continuously motivating.

Thanks for supervising me as I chop and throw with razor-sharp blades and mess around with chainsaws. A very special thank-you to the Green Angel Woodchoppers. Getting up early to spend the morning woodchopping for the community is always one of the highlights of my week. I value the stories, passion, and shared knowledge we exchange at the wood pit and at post-woodchopping coffee. Especially Dave Hargreaves, thank you for your care and dedication to making a better community.

Thank you to everyone who follows my journey online. It's been a wild ride. I never thought this path was possible, and I'm so grateful to be where I am today and it's because of your support. A special acknowledgment to the communities of outdoor enthusiasts, environmentalists, survivalists, and woodchoppers. Your shared wisdom and dedication have created a supportive and inspiring network that has been invaluable throughout this journey. Thank you for your tips, tricks, and encouragement.

Finally, to the readers, thank you for picking up this book and em"bark"ing on this journey with me. Whether you are a seasoned woodchopper, a weekend camper, or simply someone with a curiosity for these skills, I hope this book provides you with valuable insights, practical knowledge, and a deeper appreciation for the blades, wood, and fire that are integral parts of how we can live more simply and more deeply connected to nature.

ABOUT
THE AUTHOR

Nicole Coenen, an acclaimed former filmmaker, has seamlessly transitioned from the cinematic world to the rugged outdoors. She is best known as the axe-wielding, tree-climbing, maple syrup–chugging, Lesbian Lumberjack of the internet. She brings a unique blend of storytelling and outdoor adventure to her audience, which has grown to 6 million across social media platforms. Not only does she use her media presence to entertain and encourage people to step into the great outdoors, but she also works to promote advocacy for LGBTQ+ issues and environmental sustainability practices. In her community, she is involved in various groups and projects that focus on connecting people with their local ecosystems, whether to promote further protection of these areas or to help people have fun in the outdoors. Her philosophy is that nature is a place for everyone, and everyone has a place in nature.

When Nicole isn't chopping wood at the community wood pit, training for logging sports, running local outdoorsy workshops, or renovating an axe, you can find her travelling through the coastal towns and mountains of British Columbia, Canada, with her adventure dog, Bambi.

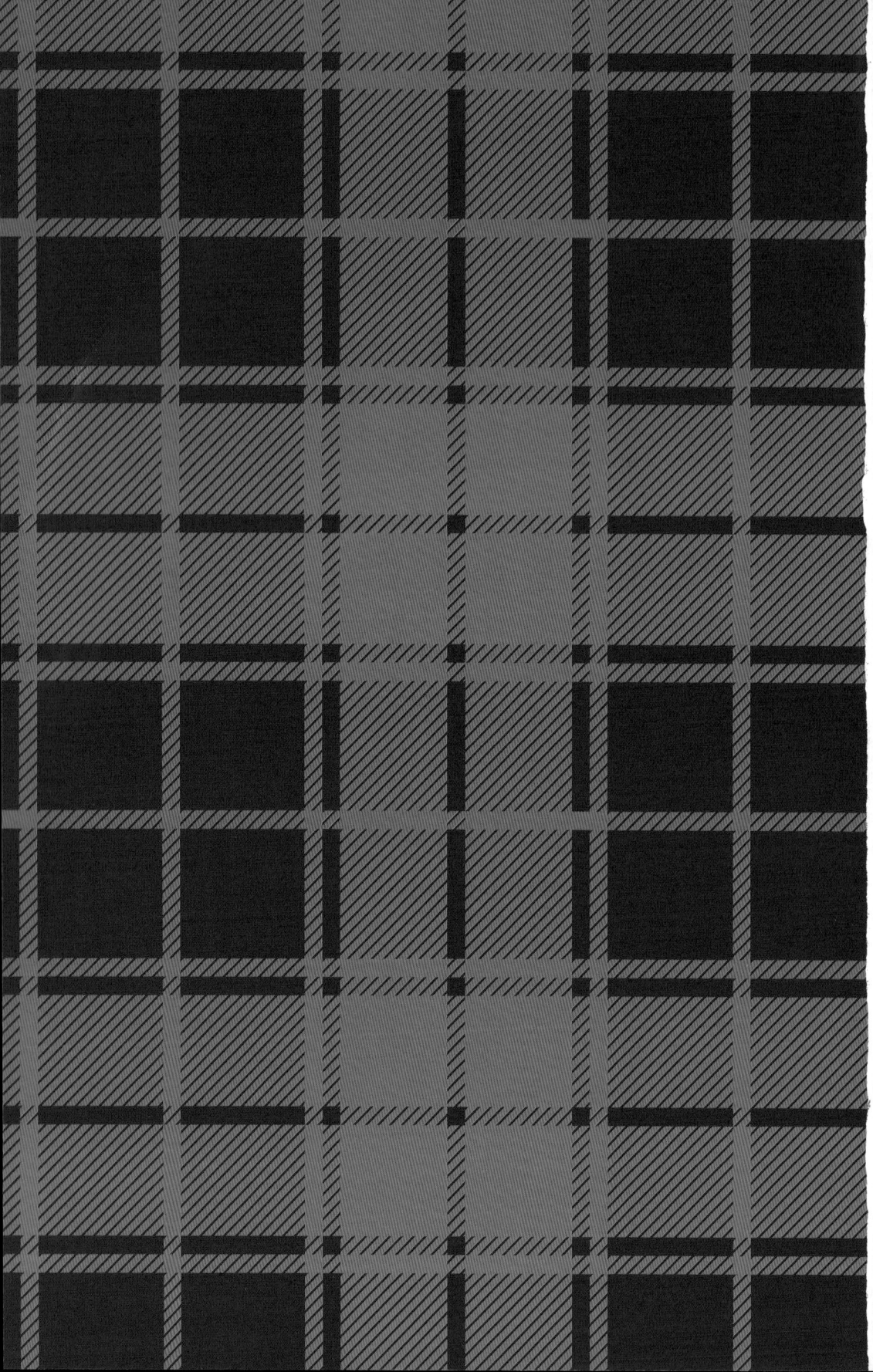